MUTUAL C

C000157295

A manual of depth pastoral care, particularly for study and use in intimate Christian communities and groups, extending the range of their accurate empathy, by including recent findings about fixated foetal experiences during early intrauterine development, and drawing attention to the presence of Christ-crucified and risen, with us, for us and in us, as the transforming power able to reconcile all human affliction

Frank Lake

Edited by
Stephen M. Maret

Foreword
Thomas C. Oden

Emeth Press

Mutual Caring
A Manual of Depth Pastoral Care

Library of Congress Cataloging-in-Publication Data

Lake, Frank, 1914-
  Mutual caring : a manual of depth pastoral care ... / by Frank Lake ; edited by Stephen M. Maret.
      p. cm.
  "Particularly for study and use in intimate Christian communities and groups, extending the range of their accurate empathy, by including recent findings about fixated foetal experiences during early intrauterine development, and drawing attention to the presence of Christ-crucified and risen, with us, for us and in us, as the transforming power able to reconcile all human affliction."
  Includes bibliographical references and index.
  ISBN 978-0-9797935-8-5 (alk. paper)
  1. Prenatal influences--Psychological aspects. 2. Maternal-fetal exchange--Psychological aspects. 3. Personality development. 4. Personality--Religious aspects--Christianity. 5. Pastoral counseling. I. Maret, Stephen M. II. Title.
  BF720.P73L35 2008
  253.5'2--dc22
                                                    2008055838

Dedication

To my beloved Friends of the Communities of Celebration, at Post Green and at the Cathedral of the Isles on Cumbrae, and others, as at South Park, Helsinki and Calgary, who have learned to give to each other this deep mutual care, and who embody the vision for its gradual extension, as the Spirit leads.

Contents

Two models: Integrate vs. Cast Out
The Need for Confrontation
Guile Must Go First

Foreword

When I first read Frank Lake's huge tome on *Clinical Theology*, I was forever changed. When I heard him speak on the passion of his last years, on the therapeutic recovery of prenatal consciousness, I was at first cautious, then curious, and only after much study thoroughly convinced. Now that I have seen the mature statement of his methods, I am all the more convinced.

Frank Lake has written a book that will be extremely valuable to practicing psychotherapists, because it shows how prenatal consciousness can be accessed in therapeutic relationships. It will also be enormously valuable to practicing pastors and Christian counselors, because it shows how exactly the therapeutic process relates to key themes of classic Christian teaching, particularly atonement and justification.

I first met Frank Lake in Oxford in the late seventies at one of his remarkable summer seminars where he had asked me to speak. I found him to be a great human being of exceptional warmth and insight, who had mastered not only the ideas and practical skills of psychiatry but also the spirit of classic Christian teaching. He was unlike any other integrator of psychotherapy and Christianity that I had ever met --- more depth, more specificity in his therapeutic strategies, along with much deeper insight into scripture and classic Christian tradition. I had come to this conclusion long before meeting him through reading his great tome *Clinical Theology*, the most important contribution of the last century for the integration of psychotherapy and Christianity. In person I realized that there was nothing phony or shallow in his way of working with patients and believers at the deepest level of their consciousness and relationships.

I commend the splendid work of Stephen Maret. Readers will come away with treasures old and new.

Thomas C. Oden
General Editor, *Ancient Christian Commentary on Scripture*

Preface

Frank Lake began writing this book as he was dying from inoperable cancer in the spring of 1982. In the two years prior to this work, he had written and published two books which addressed the topic which was his final obsession and passion, the prenatal origin of human personality. This present book is the third and final work in a trilogy which includes the previously published *Tight Corners in Pastoral Counselling* (1981) and *With Respect: A Doctor's Response to a Healing Pope* (1982). As Lake writes in his introduction to this manuscript, he believed that this third and final book was needed to tie up some loose ends and bring closure to his life's work. All three books address the issue that Lake had become convinced was the most important one for any adequate and accurate understanding of human personality formation and function. It is in this final book that Lake's thoughts take their most direct, and perhaps most radical form. He asserted that not only is the origin of human personality, and consequently psychopathology, found prior to birth, but was likely formed within the intrauterine dynamics of the first three months of pregnancy.

He had arrived at this premise gradually, and as he has written both in this book and elsewhere, somewhat reluctantly. Asserting the primacy of the first trimester as the most important period developmentally was, and still is, outside the mainstream in psychiatry and developmental psychology. But Frank Lake often evidenced an admirable openness to ideas outside the "mainstream", whether medically, theologically or psychologically. He followed his evidence, and that evidence increasingly pointed to the crucial importance of prenatal experience, particularly during the first trimester. Lake's evidence, whether the initial utilization of LSD as a therapeutic agent or the later data which came from the primal "mutual care" workshops, has been and can be critiqued as flawed and potentially problematic. But many others have found similarly compelling results. Indeed, much of the research data may have finally caught up with Lake's theories, as numerous studies over the past several decades have confirmed the importance of the prenatal experience on post-natal functioning.

A distinctive part of all of Frank Lake's books (and certainly true of this one) was his consistent attempt to blend a spiritual and theological perspective with his psychological and psychiatric one. Indeed, this was his original agenda when he founded the Clinical Theology Association and this was the underlying foundation of his first book, *Clinical Theology* (1966). Among those in the 20th century who have attempted this integration, Thomas Oden (1983) has referred to Lake's work as among "the most exemplary" (p. 9). For all of his professional career and even as his psychiatric and psychological theories evolved, Lake's primary concern was always the pastoral and therapeutic application of his theories to actual suffering individuals. As such, Lake's theories, however much critiqued and criticized, always stayed grounded in "real-life" application and always conveyed compassion for the affliction and distress of specific and "concrete" persons.

Those familiar with Frank's Lake's previous books will find in this present work all the passion, fervor and zeal that makes reading Lake simultaneously stimulating and somewhat irksome. Geoffrey Whitfield, one of Lake's contemporaries, has accurately described him as "a most exasperating but inspiring role model" (Whitfield, 2007, p. 11). That this was true in his interpersonal relationships has been noted by many. Frank Lake was a man who provoked strong reactions from people, and he continues to have such an effect through his books.

Lake could also be tenaciously single-minded. Once he latched on to an idea or theory, he would typically pursue it with dogged determinism, at least until a new one came along to displace the first. Because he committed himself to his theories with the evangelistic fervor of a "true believer", he could be impatient with anyone not as fully "on board" as he was. Since he brooked very little disagreement or questioning, his single-mindedness could often appear as narrow-mindedness. Lake's certainty in the "rightness" of his ideas often resulted in a conflation of legitimate questions and concerns raised by "friends" with unfair criticisms leveled by "enemies". The net result is that Lake's writing style can at times be overly defensive and occasionally lacking in perspective, context and discipline. This is certainly characteristic of parts of this book.

As is true with all his books, Lake's writing style can be repetitive, overly wordy and rambling. His presentation and structure are at times disorganized and excursive. It is well to remember that Lake was dying from cancer and in and out of consciousness as he labored to finish writing this book. Yet, as many have also found with his earlier writing, Lake's writing flaws are worth tolerating because his ideas are so original, creative and yes, provocative

This present edition of *Mutual Caring* is approximately half of what Lake originally wrote (about 400 pages). While attempting to faithfully represent the main ideas and concerns Lake had for his final book, some of the repetitious sections and several of the longer but less-than-relevant "excursions" have been left out. While this present edition builds on an earlier one by David Wasdell (published in 1998 and titled *The First Trimester)*, it differs significantly in that it restores the distinctly and overtly Christian tone of the original manuscript. Wasdell's edition attempted to "disentangle the psychological material from its framework of Evangelical Christian piety" (Wasdell in Whitfield, 2007, p. 77). But Frank Lake's spiritual and theological perspective was always indivisible from his psychiatric and psychological theories. This book, like his earlier ones, clearly reflects the ideas of an original and brilliant thinker, a distinctively Christian psychiatrist and theologian.

The title of this book conveys a double connotation. Mutual caring is characteristic of the healthy relationship of mother and child not only during the first trimester, but through the rest of pregnancy, birth, infancy and childhood. But where mutual caring was absent or lacking, the therapeutic relationship of counselor and counselee, of "adult self" and "prenatal self", of suffering Christ and suffering sinner, may mitigate the original lack or absence of caring. But also important for Lake is the reciprocal and mutual caring of group therapy member to fellow member, of Christian to Christian, of sufferer to fellow sufferer. Lake sees in this mutuality the hope of healing and reconciliation which, in the final analysis, was the point of this book and his life's work.

Stephen Maret
January 2009

Introduction

In February of 1982 I was discovered to have an inoperable cancer of the stomach and pancreas. A tube connecting the healthy oesophagus[1] with the small bowel made life possible on liquefied foods. Writing from my bed to friends and supporters of the Clinical Theology Association I said I felt I had another book to leave behind. *Tight Corners in Pastoral Counselling* (1981) and *With Respect* (1982) had started to address the importance of maternal tranquility or distress, for the developing embryo and foetus. An additional small book was needed to set out and summarize what we now know of the healthy and pathological psychodynamics of the first trimester (the first three months in the womb), in the interaction between the mother's emotional state and the needs of the foetus.

This new perspective changes almost everything about origins in counselling, and deepens its practice. Having spent nearly thirty years teaching that the origins of the major personality disorders lay in infancy and subsequent childhood (with birth trauma as a common-enough stress on the way), this radically changed view of the maternal-foetal psychodynamic origins to all these personality disorders is revolutionary. If it is true, our understanding of psychodynamics can never be the same again. Nor can its practice. For instance, the core of effective counselling is the provision of accurate empathy. When people experience loneliness very painfully, empathy used to have in mind a frightened baby and an absent mother. Now, however, our empathy also has to envision the likelihood that within this anxious adult is a foetal person, longing for some acknowledgement from the mother of its being there in the womb, urgently needing to know that she accepts, and does not reject the fact that she is pregnant and has a new person growing within her. The client is quick to recognize that we are living with him, within the inter-uteric world where he lies lonely and trapped.

Our whole "cognitive map" of what it is we are dealing with at depth has undergone a radical change. For instance, we have often been baffled to understand why a certain individual experiences himself at the core of his being as so utterly wretched and worthless, when his life as a baby contained no such feelings about him on his mother's part, and much that was loving. This new "cognitive map" leads us straight to comprehension when we ask what her feelings were in the first twelve weeks, when she awoke to the shocked recognition that she was pregnant, and that this "new life" was a disaster which she both feared and hated with great intensity. We must then add the implications of the fact that the mother's feelings "transfuse" the foetus, who often "knows" that it is the loathed object. Previous hints that prenatal distress percolated through into adult life have been common enough, but they have been based on snatches in dreams or fragments in free association. What we are able to offer now is a very full and well-organized account of the kind of individual and social world within which the human foetus hopes and fears, enjoys and defends itself.

For more than four years we have listened to many hours and taken full notes on twelve hundred subjects in our residential workshops. They were convinced at the time, and are even more so now when the benefits of understanding their prenatal roots are accruing, that they were actually and accurately in touch with their own foetal sensations and feelings. None of these data are offered in evidence at the bar of pure science for "proof". That is impossible and should not be attempted. However, when you listen to foetal persons undergoing the trials of the first trimester, you are struck by similar and frequently repeated statements, as well as others which flash out from their unique individual experiences. This has enabled us to reconstruct their "world" in a coherent way.

We would certainly not ourselves have stumbled upon this intrauterine scene, but for certain physical methods which we had been using for some time. These include the recumbent posture, relaxation, very deep breathing, and the use of a "journey into the imagination" which breaks through into actual recall.

Many of the subjects, however, speak of their experience as more than just therapeutic technique. They have repeatedly noted how centrally important the spiritual "ethos" of the group experience was to them. Our conviction is that we have been led into these discoveries by the Holy Spirit, who "teaches us all things" and takes the deeper resources of Christ and applies them to our deeper needs. The Holy Spirit knits together a working group, so that they are, often within a very short period of time, able to be totally honest with and open to each other. In prayer, too, people are reminded of ancient connections. Memory opens up on the injuries we have done to ourselves as well as to others. Reconciliation is opened up at all levels. That is why I have not dared to describe foetal recall in terms of a technique alone, but have embodied it in the intimate small group experience within which it actually happens.

There is another difference between this and existing forms of psychotherapy and counselling. Typically, the deeper the work to be done, the greater the skill required. I have no desire whatever to devalue the skill of our experienced facilitators in initiating the break-through; it can be vitally necessary. But once the process of recall is on the way, ordinary Christian people, who have been through the work of integration themselves, and for whom the maternal-foetal emotional transfer of distress is a simple fact of their own experience, are quite competent in a small group setting of enabling someone else who "needs work" on themselves, to get on with it. This means that the widespread development of this form of healing in Christian groups in future years does not need to wait for the provision of trained counsellors, or the conversion of non-Christian counsellors who are trained in this technique. Certainly some who have done this type of "work" many times will stand out as particularly wise and discerning, and due to their sensitivity to the Holy Spirit's prompting, very much attuned to where people are at in their growth and thus to what they need. The Christian "family" is capable of organizing this work and carrying it through in its own life. That is why "mutual help" and "mutual caring" are keynotes of this work.

So many Christian communities, which begin with high hopes, have come to grief because of intractable difficulties in human relations. Prayer and fasting have often not eased tension for long. Two people, or two families, or two factions, just cannot get along with one another, often bringing out the worst in each other. Consequently, some leave the community in the hope of finding a less constricted and confused environment. The crisis in those that remain is often a loss of confidence in Christ's power to build His own Body. Their faith in the community that has been the source of so much shared richness of the Spirit's gifts is shattered. Because the members cannot stop attacking one another, failure is built where victory had been claimed and expected.

What we have found is that the place of origin, rootage and storage of these violent fixated emotions is almost invariably found in foetal emotions of great intensity. Regression also has its part to play, because those in conflict have often disobediently allowed themselves to lose contact with the healthy, adult life of the group. They are thus left with only seeing themselves and others through their "foetal eyes". One of the happiest, predictable results of this work of "giving a voice" to the hurt or enraged foetus, is the disappearance of the old tensions between husband and wife, between family members, between families and factions, between leaders and those they lead.

All this constitutes such a radical departure from all that has gone before that it seemed necessary to write this short book to set it out. Previously, psychodynamic theory, which focused almost exclusively on post-natal life, has developed by learned discussions between the schools of thought. I myself took part in these discussions for over twenty-five years. But because of our emphasis on prenatal experience, our findings break across those earlier discussions. We seek to take the discussion up again, greatly illuminated, by incorporating the experience of foetal persons, who have been molded by their earliest and very diverse experiences, and then appear at birth and begin to respond to the mother and father in the post-natal scene. Pediatricians have often remarked on the vast differences in the way in which neonates react to an ordinarily loving mother, from acceptance to anxious clinging to sheer aversion. Our model makes it clear why these differences must exist.

Mental health experts have pointed out that there remains a lack of research in the field focusing on etiology, on the causes of the conditions psychiatrists, psychologists, social workers and counsellors energetically treat, largely by tranquilizing the mental pain. If one is concerned with understanding the origins of psychopathology, with a desire to promote widespread prevention, this lack of research is singularly unhelpful. Our findings precisely address etiology. If we wish to prevent extensive pathology, we must provide a foetal existence bathed in maternal peacefulness and even delight, where now the pathology is a by-product of the mother's severe distress.

Those who came to these astonishing findings through our workshops, as well as many women who have been sensitive to the new life within them from the beginning, have no difficulty at all accepting that these things are so. The problem is for the professionals and others who register horror at the very possibility that such might be the case. But I doubt that this book will convince where the opposition is itself partly unconscious and partly deeply invested in current theory and long-established practice. Freudian, Kleinian, neo-Freudian, objects relations, or any of the numerous other theoretical approaches are all true at their own levels, but also often hold assumptions which preclude the very idea of foetal experience and learning.

Many people have told me that they have been praying that I would be given the time and strength to complete this short book. These past few months since February of this year have been extraordinary in their way. Parts of my days have been spent in deep stupourous sleep, followed by another four or five hours of profuse sweating. This in turn has at times left me with a sense of being cleansed and energized, my mind clear and organized, ready to write steadily for eight or ten or more hours without fatigue or sagging of spirit. For those who have been a part of this prayer effort, I am most grateful. So now it is May and this volume is completed. There was talk of another volume, but that is not for me. Though my mind is clear and active, my body is rapidly losing strength and I have a happy sense that my life-work is completed. There is nothing now to keep me here and so much that beckons joyfully from "the other side". It has been a good life, and from the many, very moving letters some have written me, it is evident that many have been sharing this good life with me.

Keep close to Christ, as the person whose life within you is the source of all the creative activity that has an eternally-lasting quality. Keep close to the Body of Christ, the Christian family. Build up its life from depths examined and purified in these new ways. It has potentialities for growth within itself and for a service of healing in the wider community in the years ahead that is unprecedented in its depth and outreach. It is my hope that this small volume will set out clearly some of the reasons for that hope and draw those who are attracted by these possibilities to join with others of like mind to explore them together.

Frank Lake
May 1982

[1]Lake used the British spelling of this and other words (behaviour, centre, colour, counselling, favour, fervour, foetal, foetus, honour, labour, neighbour, rigour and Saviour).

1

The Conceptual Framework

I have no need to take back anything that was formulated about trans-marginal stress in 1966 in the tome Clinical Theology (1966), nor in the pamphlets derived from it that have been the diet of the Clinical Theology Association seminars over the past twenty years. I find it all, still, astonishingly true, well-conceived as theory and practice, and relevant resource material for Christian Pastoral Care. What I do have to admit has turned out to be a serious mistake was the assumption that the nine months of foetal development in the womb were free of significant incident, a blank without possibility of psychodynamic content. Four years of research into foetal experience, especially in the first trimester, and the records of twelve hundred self-authenticating explorers, each investigating some common area and also bringing back some highly individual finding within this subterranean world, have totally broken open the bland assumption of prenatal bliss, or, as the abortionists would have us believe, of a merely biological product with none of that self-awareness which we call personhood. Foetal life is not drifting on a cloud. It is as eventful as the nine months that come after birth. The foetus is not unaware of itself, or of the emotional response of the mother to its presence, but acutely conscious of both and of their interaction.

The Post-natal Paradigm

In the years preceding the 1966 tome, and until we began to explore pre-natal psychopathology, the main place and developmental sphere of origin for the occurrence of transmarginal states, (or, to use other terms, for the "discontinuous responses to continuous stress, when prolonged beyond a point determined by the organism", in Dollard and Miller's terminology [1939; 1950]), had to be the first half of the first year of life. We found a great deal of confirmation for this in our own records of the results on babies of failure to affect maternal bonding soon after birth. We met it also in the appalling loss of faith, hope, and love. The result was a conviction of faithlessness on the parents' part, with a despair of making any progress into selfhood and a matching sense of un-lovability, in those subjected to the rigours of restricted attention, as popularized among maternity nurses by a sadistic doctor called Truby King (1919; 1924; 1940). He was knighted for his services in giving clear consciences to coldly professional nurses and mothers who had too much else to think about and disliked cuddling babies anyway. These postnatal catastrophes could be conclusively shown to be occasions on which transmarginal reversals took place. Sudden reversals took place, from "hysterical" clamoring for the mother to come and give comfort and restore peace by her presence, to a sudden flip of all the life switches, where the pain tolerance limit was reached, into "schizoid" terror of the mother, demanding only that she keep her distance, the baby driven to distraction to avoid her touch, that had so recently been longed for. It is now no longer consoled by the closeness of others. It is happiest when left alone to find whatever goodness can be discovered, by introversion of the heart turned in upon itself and the mind ceaselessly active in compensatory fantasy. There is ample evidence that a rich fantasy world can be constructed by the infant imagination.

Those were the days of Kleinian (1948; 1957; 1975) and neo-Freudian ascendancy, when the best of British psychodynamic writers, including Fairbairn (1952; 1954), Guntrip (1961; 1969; 1971), Balint (1957, 1959, 1965, 1968), Winnicott (1957; 1958; 1964; 1965), the Robertsons (1971; 1982; 1989) and John Bowlby (1969; 1973; 1979; 1980) were focusing on problems generated by mishandling of the intimate mother-baby relationship. None of them took up our insistence that all our severe and endemic hystero-schizoid personality difficulties could most elegantly, economically and accurately be accounted for by seeing them as mirror images, exact reversals of each other's perspective, on either side of and in flight from the moment of supra-maximal pain, or dread. This hypothesis, which we have not been able to nullify, stands, in my view, stronger than ever, and is immensely fruitful in therapeutic discussion and germinal in interpretation. Needing a bit of respectable cover, we, however, like them, remained with our sights trained on the conditioning of babies and infants. This means, of course, that when we read Simone Weil (1951) or Soren Kierkegaard (1938; 1941; 1946) or the poets, particularly such anguished pieces as found in Gerard Manley Hopkins' "terrible sonnets" (1967), we tried to picture them as describing events which had happened to them as babies, or at least as no further back than the birth process. Prenatal life was, by shared assumption, presumed to be a blissful state.

Pre-Natal Grounding of Affliction

Now, having amassed a wealth of detail from early intrauterine life, its vicissitudes and typical sensations and reactions, we are able to recognize that many elements of these classical descriptions of affliction refer to the first trimester, and not at all (unless by failure of repression of the primal material, "contaminating" the post-natal scene) to the problems of the "nursing couple". For instance, Simone Weil's recurrent metaphor of the nail piercing the navel, sees it as being like a moth, pinned alive into an album as a specimen. Since it is this image which expresses the focal terror for those who "resonate" to it, it is this image, of the transfixed self, which has to be the starting point for any remedy that pastoral counselling, discerning how the Cross of Christ relates to it, can validly offer. To start elsewhere would be to be condemned to irrelevance. Simone Weil (1951) wrote:

> He whose soul remains ever turned in the direction of God while the nail [of threefold affliction, bodily, mental and social, all of which she insists act together in this state] pierces it, finds himself nailed on to the very centre of the universe. This point of intersection is the point of intersection of the branches of the Cross. (p. 135)

The nail, spear or dagger metaphor, as descriptive of the sensations of the foetus as the mother's sharp distress penetrates its vulnerable body, is exceedingly common when subjects are reliving a distress-invaded first trimester. It is never found as a metaphor arising out of or associated with post-natal deprivation, or out of any catastrophe occurring after the umbilical cord has been cut.

Kierkegaard's image of a poisoned environment spreading its poison into him until his own life and whole existence is poisoned, occurs commonly in the transcripts of our "mutual caring" group sessions from those "reliving" their first trimesters. Post-natal existence, having at least cut the cord, is not vulnerable to toxic invasion in the same way. He wrote (1938):

> The whole of existence frightens me, from the smallest fly to the mystery of the Incarnation; everything is unintelligible to me, most of all myself; the whole of existence is poisoned in my sight, particularly myself. Great is my sorrow and beyond bounds; no man knows, only God in heaven, and He will not console me. (extract 275)

There are lines in Gerard Manley Hopkins which closely correspond with the kinds of descriptions people give and the metaphorical realities they try to communicate as they undergo the experience of being invaded by a bitter melancholic (literally, black bile) flood, which pervades the flesh of the whole body, brimming over in the bloodstream carrying its curse with it. Hundreds of our subjects have used these images to express the foetal experience of being invaded, through the umbilical cord, by the black or green distress issuing from the mother's circulation, replete with catecholamines, the emotional transfer biochemicals of severe and bitter distress. These lines can only refer to this first trimester phase of human development. Though it may, of course, persist throughout the whole of the nine months of pregnancy, this is not common. Usually there is some relief in the middle trimester. Here are Hopkins' (1967) lines:

> I am gall, I am heartburn. God's most deep decree
> Bitter would have me taste: my taste was me;
> Bones built in me, flesh filled, blood brimmed the curse. (p.101)

It could be an important resource, for the recognition of these first trimester catastrophes, and consequently for our ability to provide those who suffer from them with accurate empathy, with an empathy that can now be, for the first time, fully accurate (since it is responding with a clear knowledge of when and where and how the sensations and feelings and images complained of took their origin) to search "the poetry of the schizoid", and "the theatre of the absurd" and the literature, such as that of Rilke or Camus, which sets out to transfer these pre-verbal images into exquisitely accurate words. It is all there, fully documented, but until now we have not known when human beings were undergoing the experiences, so terrible as to warrant tortured language of this intensity. Now we do, the extension of the counsellor's ability to provide accurate empathy, which is the core of his or her effectiveness, has reached a new and authentic, because self-authenticating, depth of precision.

The New Dimension

This is so new and unfamiliar, so revolutionary for our thinking about the psychodynamic origins of the commonly occurring personality difficulties to which we give diagnostic labels, and of the psychosomatic disorders that flit around them, or become the syndromes that warrant the diagnostic labels of the "psychosomatic disorders and diseases", that it seemed best to give a thorough guided tour of this strange country. The effect on me has been to give a new dimension to my seeing of the world of psychodynamics in which I lived and moved vigorously and had my being for the first twenty-six of the now thirty years of my psychiatric life. That dimension took some time to establish itself, but the steady flow of information, "from reliable sources", has proved irresistible. Now with my colleagues and hundreds of those who have participated by making the journey and spying out the land, I live, as they do, in an enhanced psychodynamic universe. The old is as true a picture as ever, but the absolutely solid reality of the new, embodying the astonishingly rich vicissitudes, responses, and interactions of foetal life, cannot fail to highlight the deficiencies in depth and shading, and in clarity about the inner structure and texture, of the post-natal picture as it has hung on the walls of our minds for so many years.

Resistance and Denial

Knowing my own resistances, when these shocking facts began to emerge, I do not imagine that the mere existence of this information about the vicissitudes of the first trimester will compel counsellors to rush to recognize this level of traumatic fixation in their clients, and utilize its detail in sharpening the accuracy of the interpretations on which empathy is ultimately based. One can only fully empathize when one can conceive of the strange images, sensations and emotions which the client is impressing upon you, utterly real to them, as referring to experiences that actually happened.

   If the whole thing is just a sick and disordered fantasy, one may struggle to empathize with that, as existing in its own right. But if we cannot conceive that any distress of that order of intensity could ever actually have happened to anybody, then our empathy, still struggling to stay with the deluded person, becomes in a way disengaged from the fantastic stuff. They are reporting their experiences as if they were based in sufferings that they had actually undergone; whereas we, the counsellors appointed to know such things, "know" that this could not be so. There is a real break in empathy here, but one we have learned to accept when counselling people we believe to be deluded or lost in illusions. Our clients sensed our spreading disbelief, and either gave up trying to communicate with us, or, not wanting us to feel useless, kindly continued to offer themselves and their material as real for them, though manifestly not a shared reality with the counsellor. This put a big strain, from the client's point of view a blight, on the counselling relationship. It can only be repaired if they learn, under firm pressure from the counsellor, to disbelieve what had been their own deepest convictions of personal reality, and trust that the counsellor, being as such an unquestionably healthy and wise person, must be correct. So they struggle to model themselves on the counsellor's disbelief. The client is inevitably split by this endeavor.

But perhaps it is not so bad after all, if the betrayal of the experiences that had made them feel so painfully isolated enables them to rejoin the human race, assisted by the counsellor, determined to believe that what they had been striving to conceive in adequate words, is to all sane people, quite inconceivable. Society offers stern alternatives here, either submission, upon which it will begin to give comfort, support and esteem again, or non-submission and the sure knowledge that this leads to an isolation that is, and is meant to be, corrective, punitive, judgmental, dismissively critical, socially disapproving to the point of crossing off the name of the stubborn rebel from the lists of those recognized as members of society. It is a heavy choice.

Of course I cannot command anyone's acceptance of the "thus-ness" of the foetal world as we have discovered it. It is possible for intelligent people to reserve final judgment on it, and yet be willing to suspend disbelief, so that they begin to be able, without constant interruption from the matter-of-fact world, to live within this unfamiliar realm and really belong to it, much as many of us did when we surrendered to Tolkien's Middle Earth in the Lord of the Rings (1954a; 1954b; 1955). That is, scientifically, a very dubious proceeding. But nowadays we are coming to realize that science itself is a very dubious proceeding, arrogantly dismissing into irrelevance for our search for truth, most of those essentially human, value-laden and true-feeling-laden experiences, which are the richest part of our human inheritance.

Professional folk have a dodgy way of blocking their own approach to matters of deep importance of which they are, to a close observer and at times to themselves, frankly so afraid as to be "scared stiff". They solemnly declare that nothing of scientific value could be derived from investigating such morbidly subjective stuff, while running their personal lives tossed around by a succession of romantic pressures and pet aversions. It is my hope that access to the sobering reality of foetal life, to that "unconscious" which, unrelated to its actual historical roots, is truly terrifying, particularly for the transmarginal elements that make death so longed for, will provide for many people those insights into their own world of limbo which will enable them to grasp, courageously, the images of unmitigated fear. Then, looking again at them with foetal vision, they may find them so comprehended and lovingly approachable as to take the entire deadly sting out of the fear, becoming reconciled to it as an old friend, of whom, in the dark, they had once been terrified.

The Problem of Verification

As we speak confidently of the extraordinary detail of recollection, purporting to be genuinely what our subjects were actually sensing and feeling, when they were embryos up to nine weeks from conception or foetuses thereafter, the reader who has not been a member of a workshop, nor been present when someone is working at this level, must want to cry halt and ask how we can be so sure.

When what our subjects discover on their prenatal tour matches closely a lifetime of psychosomatic patterning of distress, specific to this person, the hypothesis of actual origin here within twelve weeks of conception is greatly strengthened. Another aspect of verification is to observe the effect of this reliving, using the ability gained from adult and Christ-like strength, with the cognitive grasp provided by this "map", of what is happening. This makes it possible to bear the original onslaught, and therefore not to need to displace it, and further, to open up the ancient areas of containment of pain to full and vigorous expression. When, as is typical, the effect of full primal re-enactment is to modify the symptoms profoundly and in some cases cut them off at the source so that they cease, the scientific duty to attempt the further nullification of the hypothesis before announcing it has perhaps gone far enough.

The most convinced person is usually the subject. His closest relations are also convinced, as they find him or her now able to revise many life-long, automatic refusals, totally out of the power of will formerly to change. In their place comes acceptance on many levels, from God Himself to the noise of the neighbor's house next door. Many frankly paranoid projections will be withdrawn, examined, recognized, "depotentiated", and reallocated to where they really belong. Then, it is the suspicions that are suspected and a new power to trust blossoms.

Imprinting and the Origins of "Memory"

Alongside the question of verification is the embryological one. Is it physiologically conceivable that the cellular and primitive body-brain functions of the organism at six to twelve weeks can cope with tasks as complex as these findings infer that they can? Further, taking it all back to conception, is it conceivable that in the protein molecular structures of that single cell, there is the capacity to react to internal and external, good and bad, pleasurable and noxious stimuli? That the single cell can do so much is evident to anyone who has studied the analogous single-celled amoeba. We watch them expand their pseudopodia to enjoy a congenial medium, then suddenly draw in, and even encysting when the environment changes to an uncongenial one. Can a single cell also code these experiences in some way, storing primitive experience? There is evidence it can.

Richard Dryden, an embryologist, writes in *Before Birth* (1978):

> It is possible that the zygote contains information in addition to that stored in the nucleus. There is indeed evidence that the cytoplasm of the fertilized egg contains information that is essential to at least the early stages of development....There are several sites where cytoplasmic information may be stored. The abundant free ribosomes may carry developmental information. (p. 144)
>
> The mechanism of protein synthesis lends itself to analysis by information theory, with...the ribosomes helping to convert the coded message into a protein molecule. (p. 143)

When one cell divides into two and goes on dividing, as the genetic nucleus does, to reproduce that same coded information in all successive generations as a permanent record, does the cytoplasm do the same? Why not? Dryden's account implies it. The coded information must also be open to revision, as new experiences, further down the line, call for a decoding of the original message and its recoding to take account of impressive new experiences, either strongly confirming the first or calling it into question. That is to say, are there, can there be, in some protein molecular structures such as the ribosomes, not only recording capacities, but transmitting capacities? This would allow for the significant information present in the zygote to be still present in every cell of the blastocyst, and after implantation, to be carried into every cell of its enormous ectodermal invagination. This would also allow for this "data" to be transmitted to the primitive brain, which is beginning to be recognizable in a couple of weeks. These neural precursors must be capable of transferring coded data, as cells divide and differentiate, maintaining the continuity and identity of this particular organism in time. This "proves" nothing to pure science. It does show that analogies exist.

Uterine scanning from very early on in intra-uterine life observes characteristic response patterns in individual foetuses, predictably present on successive scans. Our work asks only that this observable transmission of what could already be called, not just characteristic response patterns but character, should not be curtailed at any arbitrarily-chosen week further back in embryonic life. The structural continuity of cellular formation, whether simple or complex, is firm, back to the zygote. Our work indicates that those cells have coded content, which, present at conception and added to along the line, is carried through when there are a million cells within the same organism and when there are thirty million. Every cell, endodermal and mesodermal, the guts and the muscles must, of necessity, carry the message. The specialist at transfer becomes more complex in its structural organization, capable of more differentiation of function, retrieval and storage; it does not lose contact with its earlier, simpler records. They are, as it were, in the central record room, valued as the earliest historical records available, the first impressions of the first arrival of what is now a vast community. Viewed this way, it is the insistence on any arbitrary cut off point that is physiologically improbable. Too much evidence points the other way, for the fact of continuity, from the first until whatever stage of complex present integration has been arrived at.

The Credibility of Recall

Supposing continuity of "memory" to be a fact of foetal physiology, it has certainly become unconscious. How credible is it that we have tapped in on each stage, back to the first cell, making memory at each stage available to consciousness?

In one sense, our case stands on the sheer force of cumulative evidence. The scientific method, or one of its classical ways of establishing a hypothesis, is not to try to prove it, that is often logically not possible, but to see how long it stands up to attempts to nullify it. Each person who joins a workshop and, when his or her time comes, lies down on the mat to begin the pre-natal journey, would nullify our hypothesis, cast doubt on the whole thing, if nothing happened. Very often, as they are preparing to begin, someone, knowing the strength of their own defenses will say, "Well, I bet it doesn't work with me". At times when I am working with an entirely strange group, say in Sweden, I tell myself it won't work with any of them. That consistently over ninety percent do find this a reliable way of homing in on their own pre-natal existence, from conception to bonding, with a marked tendency in the whole group to localize distress and dramatic conflict in the first trimester, constitutes a very high level of unsuccessful attempts at nullification. The hypothesis will not crack. So, it stands.

The Scientific Question

The immediate "scientific" question is, "Is it replicable elsewhere with the same results?" The answer is, "Yes, so long as you don't try to cut any corners". It would be fatal to replication to omit, for instance, the deep togetherness that happens in the group, as a result of the two days of leisured introductions, in which each person has had opportunity to speak of the life-problem that brought them here, with total freedom to be emotionally honest, and then to recollect and speak of the bodily sensation patterns and specific feelings which take hold of them when the ancient affliction strikes. That means the concentrated, respectful attention given, to each member, by the whole group, in what can become quite a marathon. This creates the utterly certain base-line for deep work, the knowledge that everything will be attended to and taken seriously, and that "everything is usable".

To say to a group of scientific workers, totally unused to having that quality of intimacy and mutual openness with the subjects of their highly "controlled" experiments, "You cannot cut this corner or you are failing to replicate the ground rules of the workshop", is to state firmly a limitation they would probably find it difficult to overcome. Yet when people reflect and report on what made it possible for them to be so totally undefended, so confident in sharing the deepest roots of their joy and longing, fear and pain, it is always this prior creation of a community of utterly gentle and in no way oppressive or judgmental people to which they refer.

If there are serious investigators, honestly concerned to know whether these things are as we have reported, I would advise against trying to replicate this in a "scientific establishment". It simply would not be a replication of the experiment, but something totally lacking in too many respects. But there is nothing to prevent their joining, as an unpretentious member of a workshop, open to the same constraints on loose criticism, and fully ready to share themselves and grow through the complex interaction of receiving and giving, and on the basis of this, coming to a scientifically reliable validation or refutation. To be scientific in these fields requires a stringency which the "scientific method", as practiced in laboratories, has always strenuously evaded. I would guess that "unconscious" roots to do with foetal experiences that have made "knowing-by-emotional-commitment" too painful and hazardous, and "knowing-at-an-emotionally-neutralized-distance" the only tolerable stance, have a decisive part in determining that deliberate subjective impoverishment that calls itself "scientific" but is not.

2

Developing Methodology

In the mid 1970s we extended the well-known "deep sea fantasy journey" to include moving into a spherical chamber, deep down on the left (the side from which maternal influences characteristically come) "just big enough to contain you, with a rosette-like structure on the wall with a tube you find fits snugly into the navel". When we asked "How does it feel to be here?" we were staggered, not only by the variety of the responses, but by the emotional explosiveness of many of them. The fantasy broke through into a buried experience, with powerful emotional components and with associated bodily sensations. Evidently some earlier happening was being vividly re-entered and re-lived. What began as fantasy developed into hard fact.

The Fantasy Journey

As we deliberately focused the imaging and recall of the state of affairs early on in intrauterine life, there was no loss of clarity or vividness, but rather a gain. As is well known, "fantasy journeys" are entered upon in a deep state of relaxation, present tensions having been first focused on, increased, and then set aside. The horizontal posture enhances the production of deep, right-hemispherical imagery, so people are lying on the floor or on mattresses. Also, the evocation of material beyond the usual limits of cognitive, left-hemispherical contact with life-with-a-view-to-controlling-it, is enhanced by deliberately deep breathing. So the relaxation, horizontal posture and deep breathing were part of the "technique" of entry, when we began to ask ourselves, "Why not begin at the beginning?" rather than crawl back to it. Why not tune in directly on conception and the blastocyst and see if we pick up any primitive stations still transmitting?

From that point we began to amass information, from subjects who

seemed perfectly capable of remaining tuned in to the stage of development being focused on by the conductor of the workshop. Three or four
subjects would usually be working at the same time, in the same or in
adjacent rooms. They experienced no difficulty at all in keeping pace
with the slow, unfolding account of the well-established stages of conception, blastocyst, implantation, establishment of placental connection
through the umbilical cord and on into the sixth, eighth, twelfth week
of intrauterine growth. They kept in touch with the others, while at the
same time sensing and giving emotional expression and a voice to their
own, quite individual, experiences while in each successive phase.

An Illustrated Talk

A most valuable adjunct to the task of understanding, for instance, what
the subject would look like as a four-week old, eight-week, twelve-week
or six-month old foetus, was provided on each workshop by someone
giving "a guided tour", from development of ovum and sperm, through
to mother-baby bonding, often richly illustrated by beautiful (though
tragic) coloured pictures of embryos and foetuses at every stage of development. However, it must be said that on workshops when this illustrated talk was not available, there seemed to have been no difficulty in staying with the week or month specified, and no loss of vividness of the
subject's recall of their experiences when in, or passing through, each
phase.

A Supportive Group

Each subject working had, squatting on mats round them, a facilitator
from our experienced house team, a workshop member (whose turn
would come later) who had volunteered to write down all their utter-
ances as an accurate record, and a third member tending a tape-
recorder. This unit came to have a quite separate life, in no way affect-
ed by the carryings on in neighboring groups, though responding to the
conductor's direction as to stage. About the sixth week of pregnancy,
each became so totally different, discovering their own pace and intrin-
sic direction of retrieval and re-living. I, as conductor, would "go off the
air", leaving them to explore, for the next couple of hours, the unique
features of their own record of the first trimester. Then, at a point usually clear to the long experience of the facilitator, a month by month move
forward through the middle and final trimester collected salient events,
and the often major changes of maternal-foetal relationship in the fourth

month and later, until they arrived at the birth experience. If the birth had been prolonged and difficult, there probably would not be sufficient energy on this occasion to go deeply into it. If comparatively easy, it would be relived and the sensations and emotions on arrival, and the cutting of the cord, experienced and "given a voice". On each occasion we planned to stay with the subject until bonding with the mother had taken place. If this was badly delayed and became a dreadful, trust-shattering experience, the session could be extended by an hour or more to permit its exploration. Alternatively it could form the focus of the second session.

At all points in the journey, from conception to bonding, the subject was in adult contact with their facilitator and small group. They would go out to the toilet and return, immediately in contact again with the foetal world at the point where they left it. What was striking was the ease with which this double level, foetal-adult contact was maintained.

Deep Breathing and Foetal Recall

There is often, though not always, the establishment of a characteristically deep breathing pattern, taking in huge lung-fulls of oxygen. If a subject's work is becoming shallow, the breathing also has probably become shallow. The commonest intervention of the facilitator was to say "Breathe deeply into that", or "Breathe deeply and intensify the feeling of where you are". If a place of panic is about to be entered, hesitation and shallow breathing go together. Courage to enter the fearful place is gained through the intention to breathe deeply into it and the actual doing of it. As we shall see later, this happens to be a most significant bio-feedback mechanism.

The different aspects of foetal experience tend to be split off, dissociated, and stored at safe distances from each other in the brain, lest contact be explosive. We wish to remake the connections, being well-prepared for the explosion. This too can usually be fostered by deepening the breathing.

For an explanation as to how deep breathing produces theta rhythm brain activity and promotes a conscious focusing on unconscious contents, I cannot do better that quote Kenneth R. Pelletier's *Toward a Science of Consciousness* (1978):

> Thus, theta rhythm [one of the brain rhythms recorded by the Electroencephalogram or EEG] appears to be a link between conscious awareness and subconscious imagery and associations; as such it could become an invaluable means of exploring the deep roots of mental phe-

nomena.

These studies indicate that controlled production of theta rhythm activity may be an important technique in the exploration of the phenomenology of conscious-ness.

In this interface state, an individual appears **to be able to use his conscious mind to focus upon unconscious imagery** (emphasis Lake's)....The ability to focus on unconscious processes enables an individual to formulate more creative problem solutions – taking advantage of previously unavailable information from his sub-conscious mind. (pp. 169-170)

One additional finding, regarding respiration patterns, was of significance. Respiration patterns during alpha-dominant states consisted of thoracic activity (chest-breathing) equal to abdominal activity, accompanied by a rhythmic pattern of inhalation equal to exhalation. Theta-dominant respiration patterns consisted of abdominal activity greater than thoracic activity accompanied by short, rapid inhalation and slow prolonged exhalation. These respiration patterns may become extremely useful in clinical bio-feedback practice. Patients may be instructed to use their own respiration patterns as feedback for maintaining alpha or theta dominance (p. 173).

We had stumbled on at least part of this. Our concern was for maximum oxygen input. Since most people are somewhat inadequate at freeing the diaphragm for full abdominal breathing, of necessity, we focused on that.

Incidentally, many anxious and tense people have an intense fear of allowing themselves to increase the range of their inspiration, lest Pandora's Box fly open. So they virtually hold their breath, and remain tense and anxious. As Fritz Perls' dictum has it, "anxiety is excitation with oxygen" (1973) where "excitation" is something in the background or foreground to be worried about.

Barely breathing is a recipe for sustained and chronic anxiety. There is a stage, where the anxious can be persuaded to breathe in a freer and less frightened way, with good but not maximal intake, where they experience marked reduction of anxiety. What we aim at, for the integration of recessed memory and the unconscious, is a third level of maximal oxygen input.

So we aim to establish powerful use of the whole lung capacity. This necessitates two things, the freeing of the diaphragm for full abdominal breathing, and the energetic use of the chest muscles to take a strong full inspiration, and then to ask them to "top it up". There follows a prolonged phase of exhalation. Often we picture the oxygen, the basis of all cell discrimination and discernment in the body, as passing to every cell, to seek out all well-ordered places to confirm them, and bringing forward into consciousness confused images, incompatible imaginations, the missing parts of old stuffed-away jigsaw puzzles, and the repressed conflicts that are typical of uncompleted foetal agendas.

So, for independently good reasons, we were encouraging the steady production, over several hours, of theta-wave activity in the brain. That this has resulted in our subjects being "able to use their conscious mind" to "focus on the unconscious", making previously inaccessible information available, "to formulate more creative problem solutions", is exactly what the bio-feedback scientist would have invited us to predict. I find this correlation of a technique, which we grew to adopt empirically, and a sophisticated technique worked out on bio-feedback principles, very impressive. So do most people whose antipathies have not already been engaged against the credibility of deliberate conscious access to unconscious foetal states of the person. It is difficult to give up the belief that full development of the central nervous system must have taken place before such detailed recording of experienced events can take place. But the evidence for embryonic and foetal memory, based on more primitive cerebral organization, is overwhelmingly strong.

Back to Conception

Recently we have added an opportunity to "tune in" on the emotional state of the mother and the father at the time of the conception. This is obviously a reconstruction of memories of quite a different order than that which begins with the "tuning in" to conception itself. We have found this to be valuable, often powerfully confirmatory of what we had supposed to be the case, but at times providing grounds for a radical revision of what the subject had assumed to be the case. So, after the prayer and the relaxation with which each work session begins, I will lead the four to six subjects to reflect on their mothers' feelings as she joins the father on the night of the conception. How does she feel about herself? How does she feel about having her first child, or adding to the family, or trying again after one or more miscarriages or fatal birth accidents? As she reflects about how her parents, and his parents feel about what they are about to do, does this add to her sense of its rightfulness, goodness, and enjoyableness? How does she feel about the man, probably her husband, alongside her? Is she full of joyful anticipation at being aroused by him, open to him and being entered by him? I suggest the positive "normal" or perhaps even ideal emotions as being present in her. This often leads to the most violent expressions of the contrary sort, and the sad recognition has to be admitted that this was a conception totally without love, totally not planned or hoped for, a meaningless nuisance she will not want to recognize when it makes its presence known.

We make positive suggestions about the mother's enjoyment of her own pelvic reproductive functions and the sexual act itself, to be greeted by one subject with such a delightful heightening of expectation that he or she is virtually feeling the mother's joyful readiness. At the same time the subject next to them may be feeling a dutiful religious compliance to a legitimate but distasteful regular demand of her lawful husband for his week-end sex. The adjoining subject may be convulsed with loathing at the whole pelvic sexual act, feeling the intensity of her mother's revulsion. We touch on the father's feelings too, though with less thoroughness. By experience we have come to value the contribution this makes to the total integrative task.

Sometimes the subject picks up a specific cause for deep concern and worry on the mother's part, as in one case her realistic awareness that if this adulterous love-affair, infinitely enjoyable, should lead to pregnancy, it would be an unmitigated disaster.

The Process of Integration

So as not to leave a misimpression of "instant cures", the following quite vital discriminations must be made. Having made contact with the pain of the damaged and defended foetus, the aim will be to give full expression to that pain. The adult is in good contact at last with the foetal self, whose predicament is fully understood and whose desire to be heard and "justified" parallel the adult's determination to "give it a voice". As long as fair opportunity is given, the foetus tends to trust and be patient, emerging with the encouragement of the adult who "makes the time". But if the adult, having once made contact and begun the abreactive task, decides to shut down on the foetus, it may by no means be willing to shut up. The pain continues to be discharged from the system or locality within which the hurt foetus is trapped. The vital difference now is that what had been for a while pain caringly accepted and shared, as a statement of the genuine suffering of one's own person at an early stage, is now regarded as a plague of meaningless pains unrecognized, as if nothing had been learned, most unwillingly borne, and alienated from the self as mere symptoms, to be dragged into numbness. These are just two opposing ways of naming exactly the same pains.

That is why it is a serious misuse of primal integration work to expect one or two sessions of it to provide a passport to freedom from symptoms. The people who would do that have quite the wrong attitude. They are bad at sustaining the new insight, that this is a sharing between persons, one's own foetal self being cherished by one's own adult self. When this is well understood and permission given to the foetal self, there may be a sharp increase of the outflow and expression of pain. But the last thing the correctly comprehending adult does when that happens is to miscall the pain "symptoms" and complain of their intensity. The sooner they are fully re-enacted, expressed and reconciled the better. So there is a welcome given to every reasonable opportunity to share the foetal hardship, at whatever intensity of distress it actually exists and emerges. You begin to see what is involved in a simple statement such as, "Really to be a friend is to lower one's defenses to be vulnerable to the demands of love". Or "it seems to be one of the 'laws' that the greater the openness the faster things happen". What is the most delightfully unresisted openness in one person may look admirably fast moving. Yet for those in whom the resistances from pre-natal terms are massive, what looks little better than paralysis, it is so slow-moving, can be the best possible if the direction is maintained. As Pope John Paul II's poem Schizoid has it "There is growth in hollow stagnation, your fever-shot eyes must not burn it to ashes" (1979, p. 39).

Feed-back and Re-appraisal of the Task

On each six-day workshop, it is customary for each subject to have two opportunities for a three-hour personal journey. After the first, a feedback session with their own small group goes over the salient events of the first three hours. What happened? The scribe helps to fill in already half-forgotten or misplaced detail of the more powerful or insistent themes. How far do they recognize, in the foetal states now fully and clearly relived, the source of life-long attitudes and decisions, fixed perceptions and rooted character stance and posture? Do they feel these have been sufficiently identified, explored and relived, in the context in which they were inevitable, indeed the only reasonable responses to a hostile and invasive environment, as to be able to leave them where they belong and to live free of them? Will it be possible to "withdraw the projections", no longer needing to see adult situations through foetal eyes? Or is there more to be recovered and relived before that is possible? What important areas were passed over? Were the subject and the group aware of points of pain which had been, because of their intensity, not fully entered on the first occasion? What could be done to enable a deeper and fuller acceptance and integration?

Subjects may become aware of an intolerable contrast between the adult understanding of what as a foetus he or she would have needed, as the essentials to grow by, and the sheer impossibility that this mother, in the disordered emotional state she was known to be in at the time, could have provided. They explore what they felt and did about her quite palpable hatred, vicious longings for the death of the foetus, and even plans for its abortion, as a totally abhorred "growth" that was in her, making life impossible. Under these conditions, with a valid "cognitive map", a clear adult understanding of the need to make this exploration and integration, and the clearest possible preparation in already visualizing the kind of foetal-cord-placental-maternal context where these terrors are predictably located, plans can be laid to explore the whole area. There may need to be many more such occasions. The original workshop may well open up on the need for extensive integrative work, prolonged over many months. But the goal is now clear, the means relevant, and each session's integration brings its own reward in new inner freedom.

A Question of Safety

To those who have been present on many occasions, and done their own work, the whole process feels, and is, totally safe. It is only when "establishment figures" and "trained therapists" are allowed to look over the wall, and make judgments on minimal evidence, that those who still look to the pundits for accreditation, come away made to feel that it is as dangerous as walking round a petrol dump with a lighted match. There are now a goodly number of psychiatrists, GPs, obstetricians, psychotherapists, counsellors, social workers and teachers, together with many other appropriately skeptical professionals and non-professionals who have been on the 6-day workshops. They are, at first, astonished that "it works" so invariably, but none of them comes away with the opinion that, done in this context, there is any risk of "precipitating psychotic states", or other uncontrolled "acting out".

Beyond Therapy

I speak of mutual caring, not because both are working at recovery and integration at the same time, which would be foolish to attempt, but because the one who today is being cared for, tomorrow or the next day will be providing the care. There is no class or category of counsellors, with a separate category of counsellees. That would be alien to the whole spirit and validated experience of the mutual care groups. The work of integration is tough and the confidence to do it with surety is not easily come by. Certainly one of the prime assets of the mutual care communities is that each person regularly explores their competence as an afflicted person, being assisted, by the presence of another, to affect the reliving and integration, and also of being on another occasion in the responsible assisting role.

There can be no loss of self-esteem here, as if to say, "I am always at the receiving end. I never seem to have anything to give that anyone else can use". That is ruled out by a basic practice of mutual care.

That sense of being a perpetual beneficiary, useless in assisting even one's own recovery process, is the regular, standard and inevitable outcome of the doctor-patient relationship as it is usually practiced. Counsellors evoke client participation, but they do not give to clients the clear understanding that what I have done for you today you are fully competent to do for me tomorrow. What are years of expensive and arduous training for, if not to enjoy a little well-earned one-up-manship? It would seem professionally offensive to pretend that untrained clients, out of their own experience of infirmity alone, when well-integrated, had an adequate competence to be a counsellor for someone else in a like predicament. Yet so it is, whatever resistances may be offered by counsellors as a profession.

Counsellors will continue to have a social mandate, and a recognizably useful role. They will continue to be the appointed persons who permit selected individuals to gain some private relief, within the counselling relationship, from the really quite cruel self-isolation, concealment and ruthlessly-imposed emotional loneliness, which is the standard cultural recipe for life together in conventional society and the establishment.

The remedial options open to afflicted personalities are much wider than they were in the past. Previously we could only think in terms of a vast increase in the number of skilled counsellors, not just middle-class for the middle classes, but drawn from and acceptable to the working, and often habitually non-working, class. The economics of their selection and training, and of their being made available to the community without charging their clients were mind-boggling. It seemed the only way forward, but one which would never be taken, except on a small scale, promoted and financed by dedicated charities.

It is now quite evident that the solution to the problem must arise, and does arise, from within the heart of the problem. The solution is embodied in those persons who experience it fully from the inside, and are graced with the capacity for accurate empathy out of their own painful inner experience. The transformation begins as soon as they have learned to live with it, not as a disqualification for life together, but as an opportunity with inexhaustible potential. This does not come naturally to the deflated world of the afflicted, who persistently see themselves, when in contact with their roots, as *les miserables*, "the sons of want". There must be a powerful injection of spiritual imagination, able to transcend the severely limited horizons imposed by the condition itself.

The Eastern style of transcendence is precisely inappropriate, insofar as by prime intention it intends to avoid suffering. This may be done by training people to consider suffering to be an illusion, with meditation techniques designed to absorb the mind so totally elsewhere as to distract the meditator from any memories of having suffered.

Following the clear example of what happened to the human-divine Body of Christ, through his ministry to his passion and crucifixion, we find ourselves moving in the opposite direction, into suffering and into the fullest possible experiencing and assimilation of it. When the same Body of Christ is present in the eucharistic meal, it is given to us for our nourishment, health and healing, as the broken body of the Saviour, and as his blood shed to the end point where it was so totally given as to be unable to support his own life. When the same body of Christ reappears as the community of Christians, the same quality of costly, self-giving love for others is characteristic of them. If that is not so, some other spirit of anti-Christ has got into them. They are working, not for, but against his kingly rule, where the one on the throne is the Lamb, slain from the foundation of the world. Here is the full, whole-hearted identification with the worst forms of suffering, which, because its action is freely and in total love undertaken by the Saviour, determined to bring the love of the Father to the places where it has seemed to be most absent, does constitute the exactly adequate conditions for complete transcendence. This identification robs affliction of its worst destructive powers, to humiliate, degrade and wretchedly isolate the afflicted sufferers by bringing the Son of God totally into their ancient, yet life-long misery, to share it to its last dregs.

Thus, the Kingdom of God, embodied in the Body of Christ, has a

better way to offer than mere counselling. Since all the members are gift-
ed with competence by the Holy Spirit, not all to preach or administer,
God forbid, but all to be present with each other at times of abysmal
weakness, when the afflictions of the beginning of foetal life are rising to
consciousness. They ask to be given a voice, a place of protest, and a
court of justice to point out why they have for so long refused to cheer
about the goings on in the cosmos, and have refused the optimistic
offers of the breezy evangelists of a cure-all gospel. But now, nevertheless, emerging from an abyss at the bottom of the world, they have
become reconciled to the catastrophes that did the damage, and are
now pristinely prepared to respond to the exchanges of love. I am not
here delineating a utopia that nowhere exists, but simply describing
what is happening in the communities of Christians where they are
open to these realities and wisely experienced in providing for each
other, opportunities for this quality of deep mutual care.

3

The Experiment

What follows is a plain account of what we do in our mutual care groups. The result is the ability, in over ninety percent of those who submit themselves by joining a workshop (an entirely self-selected group), to recover and relive how they felt from conception to bonding, with particularly regular force and relevance in the first trimester. Participants appear to be able to do this while keeping full adult contact with the supportive group. The method is straightforward, without any mystique which holds a secret key to some magic door into the "unconscious". The very simplicity and directness of it are reassuring.

To those who find themselves intensely interested, perhaps both personally and professionally concerned, but looking over the wall for further evidence, I would say, "Why stand outside, when that of which we speak carries full conviction only from the inside?" Let me invite you to spend some time with one of these groups for whom this foetal world is one of the common basic facts of their experience. But don't expect to find in this any more than a small part of a very full life of worship, service and happy-serious fellowship. Come, ready to make your own journey, but also be ready to be told by other group members that, for one reason or another, they do not consider you ready. The process is not a drive-in car wash. It is a delicately balanced complex of adjustments requiring mature experience and discussion, a consensus and a sense of spiritual "go ahead", if it is not to be scandalously misused.

Getting Started

Four people, or maybe six, are part of a larger group, talking together about an experiment they propose to undertake. As with any group of people at any time, were you to make careful inquiry, some are more and some are less tense than "the average". But these differences are not observable on the surface. They are all behaving appropriately, attending to each other as the occasion arises. A fairly homogeneous group of human beings, one might say.

The experiment is by way of a journey into a particular segment of each person's past life. The methods used have already been described and are based on the findings of over twelve hundred people who have submitted to the same experiment, under the same controlled conditions of a residential workshop. Common sense is astonished and may well be affronted by what workshop members assert. They claim that by this method the doors of memory are opened, in some cases so far back that they experience themselves reliving what it felt like for them to be conceived, or to be floating free in the womb as that perfect sphere, the blastocyst. Many experience what it was like to receive the inner command to "get stuck in", and to undertake the easy, or at times difficult, enjoyable or perhaps distasteful task of becoming implanted into the wall of the maternal womb. Not all of those who undertake the experiment open those very early doors. There is a stage in the experiment, however, when predictably, all their doors fly open, so that they all become vividly aware of how it felt for them to have entered this particular stage of intra-uterine existence. We open this door on their life as a five or six-week embryo.

The conductor, speaking to the whole group will say something like this:

> From shortly after implantation, you, as a tiny embryo have been making strong contact with the placenta through the umbilical cord. It is short and relatively huge. Now you have reached nearly six weeks from conception. The embryo has a large head and the nervous system is developing inside it. Little stumps of arms and legs are appearing. A strong connection has now been set up between you, the embryo, and the placenta, through a smooth, firm, umbilical cord. The placenta is firmly attached to the wall of the womb. So your circulation is in intimate contact with that of your mother. Her life and yours come close together at this point.
>
> Breathe very deeply for a while and then become aware of what it is like, for you as an embryo, to be attached to your mother, now in this sixth week.

With unfailing predictability, as many doors fly open as there are subjects working. Some are giving powerful expression to what they are experiencing, even while the "conductor" is coming to the end of his or her "directions". Most take a minute or two. Others may take five or ten minutes, needing reassurance that they are not being hurried, and that i they who are in charge of the exploration. With one in ten, some patient individual facilitation may be necessary. One person in twenty does not make it at all. There are usually clear clinical indications why, at this time and place, with their particular dynamics in the state they are, and inner and outer life supports and integrating factors being what they are, their organism has decided in its wisdom not to add the contents of the embryonic cellar to what is already a too-precarious balance. It may be asked, "Should you not have predicted this and dissuaded them?" On balance we decide not to, even though we may have had qualms. To intervene would be to transgress the fundamental rule of all this integrative work, which is that each subject takes full adult responsibility, having understood what it is that is being done, to participate or not. Once I begin to encourage or dissuade, I adopt a "parental" role and the subject is seduced into a "child" role. That is fatal to the integrity of the work. It is an important issue, worth mentioning, but not what we are here to describe.

The Language Question

As the doors to the existences of the six-week embryos fly open we are immediately astonished that no two are alike. They use language, fully aware, of course, that no such speech as they are using now was available at that time. But we have to face the fact that a pre-cursor of language is present. Not only is it present in rudimentary fashion, it is capable of carrying nuances of meaning, and changes of meaning, and the vast range of emotional states present in those six people. Each of them is convinced that what they are saying in the present is an accurate report, couched in such language as they can find, of the deepest experiences of their life. So clear and convinced are they of this as their own genuine production, they will say, "I felt that intensely then, and I can feel it just as intensely now. It has become basic to my being me. That is how I am, and that is how life is. It has become settled conviction for me that life will go on being like this. Oh I know that lots of other things happened, but this is always there, as a basic factor in my identity. I look out on life with the eyes of the foetus that I am now, seeing what I see now. So often it is stronger and surer than what my adult eyes see."

Four Levels of Foetal Response

Level 1: The "Ideal"

Most striking, when the majority are giving a voice to their own particular quality of distress, is the embryonic person who, in a world of their own, is in a state of warm and contented happiness, even of a deeply embodied (not ecstatic) bliss. They are aware that the umbilical connection with mother from the placenta is wholly satisfactory. The mother "keeps a warm womb", they may say. Or, "she is so peaceful", "there is such a sense of tenderness and love coming and going".

Should a questioner, mistaking the time-scale ask, "Does your mother accept your being there?" On several occasions I have heard the reply, "Of course she doesn't know I'm here yet. I'm too tiny. But it will be all right when the time comes".

I have placed this report of first trimester foetal joy here, to establish that the maternal context provided by the mother is, from time to time, reported as "Ideal". All the warmth and tenderness of the love she is receiving from her husband, family and neighbours, fortified, perhaps, by a spiritual sense that God the Father's exchanges of love are just like this, mix together. This mixed-together love is then made available to the foetus within her, though she may yet have only an inkling that she is pregnant. One would assume that the basis of this love comes from a foetal life and childhood of a similar quality when her own basic character formation was beginning within her mother.

Level 2: The Coping Response

When there is a failure to meet the essential foetal need for recognition and caring attention, or when the foetus is recoiling from the influx of maternal distress, we observe that the foetus, having lost hope of the "ideal", attempts to cope with the deficit or the distress, or both. An incredibly variable series of coping devices are set up, embodied in psychosomatic patterns and providing "scripts", namely, "What to do when similarly stressed". Though repressed at the time, these re-emerge with the sharpest clarity subsequently, later in womb life, during the stress of birth, in babyhood, infancy and on into adult life. This need to develop a "coping response", we are certain from all kinds of focusing evidence, begins well within the first trimester.

The coping response typically involves an acceptance of the ongoing exchange with the source person, out of sheer need, with the corollary that the "badness" must not be fired back at the placenta/mother via the excretory umbilical arteries, but loaded up in the foetus' own body structures. The unbearable badness is "coped with" by displacement into and containment within almost any part of the body, alimentary, respiratory or uro-genital tracts, muscle groupings such as the shoulder-girdle or low-back, skin and its own emotional system. This means that an ostensible ongoing acceptance of the way of exchange is riddled with ambivalence. It also constitutes an apparently necessary refusal of love or relief to those parts of the foetal body that are being used for displacement and containment. No offered love can be allowed to enter those areas to have mercy on them. This is somewhat typical of the origins of depressive dynamics. The initial disappointment of badly deficient or actually distressing input was accompanied by a desperate anger at the wrongness of it; but that rage is immediately capped by foetal anxiety at the "thought" of hurling it back at the placenta. This is a paralytic fear which leads directly to the retroflection of rage.

In pastoral practice it is now possible, working in mutually-supportive small groups, to recover these sequences in detail and relive them, with an adult presence, the person's own, supported by the others. This gives permission to the foetus to give a voice to the various original cries and pleas, knowing that they are now being heard without blame. It also invites the person to reintegrate and express the foetal rage, against the placenta/mother/mother's world, and against God. While unknown during foetal life, on the cross God clearly means to take responsibility for the primal catastrophe and offer his flesh-taking apology. We are invited to break his Body and shed his Blood. As his murderers we are still his beloved.

Foetal coping is really saying, "However hard it is to hang on to acceptance of the mixed good/bad, rough/smooth stuff that comes in at the navel, the alternative, to refuse the good because the bad is so bad, is cut oneself off from life itself". The stronger foetuses, in conjunction with the more inadequate mothers, often take up what we call the Foetal Therapist stance. They accept, as foetuses, the life-long burden of doing everything in their power to prevent their mother from being distressed. What starts in the first trimester can be controlling life fifty years later. They totally refuse to accept the meeting of their own needs.

Level 3: Total Opposition

The inability to handle the situation by coping, in the face of too severe, too prolonged, unremitting deficiency of maternal recognition of the foetal presence, leads inevitably to the next stage, that of total opposition. Or an alternate cause may be the sense of "negative umbilical affect", experienced like a great nail of affliction or skewer transfixing the foetus at the navel, with an overwhelming invasion by bitter, black, maternal emotions.

The normal innate longing, the "shopping list" so to speak, is for a steady offering of tranquil, attentive, happy emotions, via the placenta and umbilical cord, from a mother who is glad she is pregnant and who communicates with the foetus as with a person. When this is completely absent, the foetus can sometimes use the night, when the mother is asleep, to re-gather its incredibly renewable faith, hope and love, to reaffirm what ought to be and wait like Prometheus for the day when the carrion birds return to the attack. In the face of the terrible opposite of all that foetal existence should be, the foetus goes into total opposition to the invasive maternal distress. Nothing is left to indicate that the open, accepting attitude is at all possible while this invasive flood persists. The preservation of some defended bits of life, of acceptance of the validity of the longing for good in the face of total environmental destructiveness, is tantamount to refusal of all that the environment offers, while the adult is acting under the force of this foetal dynamic perspective.

The foetus, as early as the eighth to twelfth week and rudimentarily even earlier, is capable of splitting itself, displacing the incoming "shit" as they commonly call it, symbolically into one or other bodily system and there, again, symbolically or in image, containing it, or trying to. In many of the worst cases, having retreated through successive body levels, the whole body up to the neck has to be consigned to the containment of badness. The good is imaged as taking refuge in the head, or as retreating to just the centre of it. The good self may be compelled to leave the whole body. It is then felt as existing only outside the body, floating in space above the head.

As first you cannot believe this extraordinary saga, but when you have heard it emerging, independently, from dozens, even hundreds of people, the force of it penetrates even the resistant medical mind.

Level 4: Transmarginal Stress

So far we have touched on the "Ideal" situation and response, and dealt with the defective one which, nevertheless evokes in the foetus the "Coping" response, and that which is so bad as to demand total "Opposition", in order to preserve some sense of refusing the bad, so as to leave room, when the attack is over, for a return to openness. At least the oppositional stance does not break faith with the sense that the offer to which a response is asked, ought to be good.

There is, however, a regularly occurring fourth level or sphere of response. Sphere is an appropriate word, since if the organism is driven, by the sheer impossibility of keeping up the opposition to the invasive evil which seems interminable and relentless, into what Pavlov called transmarginal stress (1927), the individual has been thrust into a totally different world than those preceding it. Up to the margin, the foetus, on the side of good, has been opposing the badness, longing for relief and a better situation in which to lower the opposition. This stance is essentially life-affirming, even though, in relationship to the totally bad environmental influx, totally opposed. Beyond the margin, stressed beyond bearing, the foetus longs, not for life, but for death. The plea is not for a relief of the weight, but that it may quickly be crushed out of existence. Everything to do with fighting to live has become too painful to look at again. The only hope is to end it all. In this sphere, all that existed in the former one is reversed and totally opposed. Here is the root of the most determined refusal to seek life or let oneself be loved.

We must step back and put this extraordinary volte-face in its wider context. In my tome of 1966, *Clinical Theology*, I found it necessary to devote almost four hundred pages to this "Schizoid Personality Disorder". That other psychiatric textbooks often mention it in one or two paragraphs is attributable, I would say, though few psychiatrists would agree, to the fact that to a socially acceptable degree, the basic schizoid perceptions and behavior patterns that express them, are in fact typical of psychiatrists themselves. This is true in their relationships not only with their patients, but also with their spouses and families and with themselves. It is to this ill-recognized, but pervasively operative fourth level of distress, radically hostile to life itself, that I would attribute the significantly higher rate of suicide among psychiatrists and their spouses, higher than the rate among doctors in general, which is so much higher than that of the general community. Even at its best, the schizoid personality is condemned to exist by means of a largely intellectual defensive "false-self system". However brilliantly successful in a world where so much academic and professional life idealizes "schizoid" attitudes, hostile to warm human emotional sharing, it is always liable to break through the defenses with its seductive, deadly face. So, the mere recognition of this syndrome in psychiatric texts, with nothing to follow that indicates wide experience of "treating" or "helping" sufferers from it "feel better", simply represents facts.

Those who have penetrating insight into their own schizoid dynamics are acutely observant of those who are, like so many doctors and professionally trained role-players of all kinds, suffering from the same abysmal despair of life, but have not had the breakdown that would strip away their defenses. The primal affliction, so awful as to make death infinitely preferable, is still well repressed. Schizoid sufferers who have achieved insight know that their observation, from a point or stance underneath the defenses that others are still using, is absolutely accurate and factual. They know they need help to make their grim state of radical life-negation tolerable in a supposedly life-oriented world; but by the same insight they are assured that from whatever source it is to come, it will not be typical Health Service psychiatry that provides it. So they stay away. Moreover, their rigorous respect for the painful reality they have perceived makes the offer of drugs to dull, deny, or confuse that reality an offence against their essential truthfulness. There are, of course, millions of young people, afflicted by this same need to reject life-as-it-comes-to-them, who are too gripped by the many-leveled distress of it to achieve the pained detachment of an observer. They take to drugs, of all kinds, and some to alcohol, or both, in order, for a while, to blot out the anguish. They become careless of precautions, desperate in piling "remedies" together, for if death comes, that will be no disaster, rather a blessed end to all. What follows could not be worse. If oblivion to the body's anguish, to constant mental self-torture, and to the social self-scorn that has made commitment to the bonded exchanges of love unbearably painful were all part of the package of actually dying, that would be bliss indeed.

All this has been accurately described within the Christian tradition, with those marvels of self-observation of the condition, by Simone Weil (1951), Soren Kierkegaard (1938; 1941; 1946) and so many lyrical poets from St. John of the Cross (1949) to George Herbert (1941), Gerard Manley Hopkins (1967) and Pope John Paul II (1979) himself. Alongside them are innumerable admirable humanist poets, endowed with similar exquisite truthfulness. Though it deals with the hells of pain, this poetry has a self-transcending beauty, grace and love, expressed in the perfectly appropriate form of words. The "schizoid" poets have bequeathed a heritage that has given meaning to meaninglessness, a vibrant life to a paralytic death. Some of these poets have given broad hints that what they were in contact with was intra-uterine. William Blake's *Book of Urizen* (1966) for instance, explicitly explores these weird distortions of existence, in specific relation to the nine months of foetal dependence on the womb and on the mother who, for better or for worse, carries and supplies it. Are we now able to be more specific about the time and place of origin of this transmarginal stress?

The evidence, from the twelve hundred subjects who have now re-experienced their own particular foetal vicissitudes, from implantation to the end of the first trimester, at times spreading over into the fourth month, is that this supra-maximal or transmarginal stress takes its decisive origin at this very early stage of human growth and development. It is truly shocking to have to think of such vulnerable bits of humanity, from nothing to three inches long, undergoing distress, affliction and pain of such severity that they despair of being able to cope, despair of being able to keep up an opposition to the badness. They fall into double despair, joining the destructive force, making its ruthless power their own, turning it relentlessly against themselves. They are like a spring when it reaches the limit of elasticity and becomes overstretched. It has lost its power to return, and becomes deformed, irregular and shapeless. This, we must conclude, is what happens to the human foetus, within three months of conception, when it is invaded by an intolerable intensity of maternal distress. Can this be believed to be true?

The human race has manifestly acquired a total resistance to considering any such possibility. Only in the great classical myths, such as Prometheus, or Oedipus, (which means "swollen foot", as whose would not be, staked to a mountain), has the race permitted itself a distant view of these grim realities. The myth serves both to affirm these inhumanly cruel tortures and herculean labours, and to deny, by looking elsewhere, their actual provenance or site of occurrence.

From other medical, epidemiological and anthropological disciplines quite apart from our own research findings, the evidence of origin of the deepest or earliest distresses to which the human organism is prone, must now be conceded to be intra-uterine.

What is astonishing about the outcome of our own exploratory workshops is the availability, in over ninety percent of self-selected subjects, of specifically individual "memory", with the power to relive and re-enact events and responses, evidently coded and recoverable in great detail, related to the first trimester. In most cases the worst of the distress is confined to this period. When the subjects, guided from month to month, pass into the period, sometime in the second trimester, when typically, even women who have been badly disturbed settle down to "get on with having the baby", they report a decisive diminution of acute distress. They enter upon a quite different sphere of existence, no longer dominated by the ubiquitous harassment of the first trimester, but for the most part well able to be coped with. There is space and a new ability

to move. Indeed, from many reports it would appear that the utter ter-
ribleness of the early months has already undergone an almost total
repression. If, in the weeks just before the birth there are indications that
the foetus is distressed (and there are several well-recognized and not
uncommon conditions of disparity between foetal need and maternal
supply which give rise to this), the whole distress of the first trimester can
be re-awakened. This makes the actual condition of foetal distress at the
end of the pregnancy much harder for the foetus to bear, more ominous
and much less tolerable. If there has been a transmarginal reversal into
the death wish in the first trimester, when repression fails and it joins the
actual distress of the pre-birth weeks, this greatly increases the likelihood
that this too will become transmarginal, with the onset of a wish to die
rather than to live. The temptation to give up is experienced more
severely.

Perinatal Echoes

Birth may go well and be greatly encouraging, in no way arousing the
distresses of the first-trimester, but rather, reassuring the growing self, as
it passes into the new sphere, that more and more distance is being put
between life now and life then, with all its catastrophes. The birth struggle does, however, provide a sufficient range of traumatic emergencies,
sufficiently common, and sufficiently close to in extremis situations and
actually near-fatal terrors, for the resonance and reverberation of first
trimester crises to break through the repression into the experience of
the baby being born. Subjects are very aware when this happens that
they are reliving a difficult birth. They realize that during their actual
birth, the sudden onslaught of de-repressed distress from the past could
not be recognized as such. It had seemed to belong to the present and
had plunged the baby into a seemingly unitary experience of devastating and hopeless catastrophe. On reliving the birth as an exercise in integration, the subjects are usually able to recognize and identify the two
component parts, allocating them to their now known and consciously
remembered occasions of origin. That is to say, they know with remarkable inner clarity what actually belonged to the "obstacle race" of their
own birth, as it actually happened, and what belonged to the first
trimester, which had escaped into the distressing crisis of birth when
exhaustion and "isomorphic resonance" had broken down the repressive
barrier.

By "isomorphic resonance" I mean the greater likelihood of repressed experiences breaking through into consciousness when what is happening in the here-and-now has the same shape, or pattern, or responds to the same image as one of those which were initially suffered, split off as unbearable, and repressed. For example, a sense of total and unreasonable conviction, together with a denial of any clear indication as to what action or restraint of action is required, but in its place a total confusion of seeming clues and orders, is a common pattern, frequently encountered both in the first trimester and in the birth process as the baby perceives it. The scanning mechanism of the brain, eager under stress to uncover earlier ways in which the organism had met, and, hopefully, been able to handle this pattern of catastrophe, breaks open into the first trimester. It discovers the same patterns to have occurred on an earlier occasion. But unfortunately, during this earlier occurrence of the pattern in the first trimester, there was evidently, for week after week, no solution at all, but only despair of various intensities. So, where some people's scanning does evoke reassuring memories of similar problems to those in the present, having been soluble by this or that strategy, here there is no such encouragement available, but only a heightening of discouragement.

Our records show that even when the first trimester has been tranquil, because the mother was tranquil, in every way building up a sound foundation for a sense of self-hood, the foetus correctly picking up and responding to the mother's welcome of the pregnancy and the person now growing within her, in spite of that good start, a difficult birth can nevertheless be so devastatingly traumatic and near-fatal that transmarginal stress and the longing to escape by death can and does occur here for the first time. It is at its worst in cases of long-continued impaction, such as severely arrested labour due to a persistent occipito-posterior position. The very duration of the obstruction, under intense constricting pressure on the head hour upon hour, would drive an adult to distraction who "knew" by the fact that they were alive at the end of it, that it must have had an end. The baby, however, reflecting and sharing the panic and desperation and sense of failure of the mother as well as its own, is totally without grounds for hope and encouragement. Severe transmarginal stress does occur in such cases.

Adults who have undergone this tend to back off major transitional crises as if they had some deadly, shut-in-to-die threat implicit in trying to get through them. This may make a terror of all testing situations such as examinations. The candidate is utterly certain he will fail under testing. Hidden weaknesses will be exposed. He will forget everything he ever knew. His mind will go blank or he will panic and rush out of the examination hall. It is certain that he or she "will not get through". It won't have been worth it to subject oneself to such strains. To use a now less common word, he will be "plucked", with all that it means in terms of loss of social esteem, disgrace and total loss of face.

For many years now we have been able to transform this situation for those who suffer from it, by taking them back to relive the birth, where, to their astonishment they recognize and can re-allocate to where it belongs, every facet of their examination phobia. Knowing what it is all about and knowing that there was a successful outcome, individual subjects are able to enter and assimilate occasions of transmarginal stress which have made them, like Job, "long for death like hidden treasure" (Job 3:21). They integrate an aspect of the self that had been both terrifying and repulsive. They become reconciled to an experience which had totally, and until now irremediably, split the person. During the fifteen or more years that we have been doing this, we had no idea that a similar reconciling work was waiting to be done, in respect of catastrophic suffering in time to conception than to birth.

Shadows of Implantation

We have records of some of the strange reasons for refusing the process of birth, in which the task is to squeeze through from one sphere of existence to another, which when reached will certainly be a totally different place. Will it be a better place you enter, after the transitional effort of squeezing yourself in, or a worse one, or a totally horrific torture chamber? If the question is asked by the baby as it begins to respond to uterine contractions by squeezing its way along, as if eager to get into the next place, "Where have I been through this kind of experience before, and what was the upshot?", several subjects have been aware of picking up the coded record of their implantation. As blastocyst, free-floating in the womb, they had received the message "get stuck in". The concept of "message" is permissible since every blastocyst, having been for some days happy just to "hang about" in the womb, does suddenly evince a need, virtually a command, to stick to the wall of the womb, penetrate it during a few hours "struggle", and implant itself firmly in the maternal tissue. For many, this proves to be a good nest to have landed in, warm and well-tended, sweet, fresh and clean, an ideal place to settle down in and open up the umbilical-placenta exchange, taking in an abundance of nutrients both metabolic and emotional (probably by means of the transfused catecholamines of a tranquil mother).

For others, the transition proves to be an immediate disaster. The blastocyst had squeezed its way into an ice-box, or a cesspool, into a burning fiery furnace or a nauseating, bitter, acrimonious place. When this is the effect of squeezing through from one development phase to the next on the first occasion, the lesson learned powerfully determines what the likelihood, indeed the certain outcome, will be on any subsequent occasion. So, as the baby squeezes its way, at the end of womb life, into whatever is to follow, if the question is asked, "What will be the result of this pressured effort of mine?" the answer can be badly confused. The baby hopes to come out into a good place where all the conditions of loving recognition and acceptance necessary for growth will be present. The innate expectation of the species certainly speaks hopefully of this, as of all developmental transitions, as a time of betterment. In these subjects, that natural expectation of effort proving worth it because of all-around gains has been radically shaken. The force of the primal lesson can be so overwhelming that the innate optimism is destroyed. In its place are inserted expectations which exactly correspond to the specific lesson learned after implantation, that the place that is waiting for you is ice-cold, or filthy, burning hot or bitter.

The obvious next question is whether there is any evidence that these images and sensations did correspond with what was known of the mother's attitude, to her inner pelvic world where the womb lies, or to her outer social world where her habitual emotional responses were generated. I can remember no expectations to the response given by those who ask this historical question. Invariably they know, or can reliably infer that their mother's attitude to her inner and outer worlds was such as to give rise to these foetal images.

The kind of person she was, and the way she responded to her own body or behaved in the world, were such as could hardly fail to give rise to precisely those specific foetal horrors and their accompanying sensations and images, that had been relived just after implantation.

Says one, "My mother kept sex on ice. She was totally frigid. It has always been a mystery that she got round to letting my father impregnate her with me. All her genital and reproductive functions were totally without warmth. She certainly kept a cold womb, and I knew it as soon as I got there."

Says the second, "Mother always regarded sex as disgusting, a necessary part of life but thoroughly repulsive. Dad really cared for her and suffered a lot because of her sick revulsion towards sex. She got it from her mother who had herself been drilled, and drilled her daughters, into equating sex and reproduction with everything dirty. That is certainly what I felt I had come into as soon as I'd been implanted."

Says another, "My mother was always at war with her environment. Nothing was ever right for her. Everything, as she saw it, conspired to make her life a thing to be perpetually angry about. I remember her getting into flaming rages. Was she ever not in a temper, either seething inside her, waiting for life to play its next dirty trick on her, justifying the outburst, or in the running fight that used to go on with my father and his family that we lived with. If all those furious emotions got through to the womb, as I suppose they must, no wonder I seemed to exist in 'a burning fiery furnace.' And I didn't have Daniel's divine protection."

The fourth reports on her mother's basic response to life as bitterness. "She felt a helpless victim in a world where so many people had the best of everything. She was prone to attacks of bitter jealousy, of her husband's sisters particularly, and they weren't all that much better off. She was burned up with envy. I suppose that if I, hoping for a happy, peaceful and contented womb, landed in one who was marinated in her bitter miseries that is how I would be bound to feel about the place into which the effort of implantation landed me."

Whatever the detail, scant or prolific, there has always been, in our experience so far, ample support for the hypothesis that the womb is not an organ in a woman's body which has a unique immunity from her circulating emotions, but is party to them like the rest of the organs of the body. Nor does the placenta act in any way as a filter. Moreover, according to the general principle in psychosomatic medicine, specific organs can become the target of intense hostility and are damaged by it and their functions deranged. These wombs were no exception.

When these two lines of information have been researched and found to correspond, the shock of reliving the catastrophe of implantation providing one set of data, and the correspondence with the mother's known emotional input into the womb providing the second set of data, the subject is able to put them together. For the first time they are able to identify the source of the dire warnings and resistances that accompanied the act of squeezing oneself, necessary to getting born, namely that as soon as the squeezing was successfully over, some peculiar kind of torture chamber and its ruthless operators would take over. If, as is likely, this prognostication of disaster should push themselves forward, had crazily blocked all kinds of personal initiatives in later life and the good they were obviously leading to, they are now able to understand and integrate what had been the actual post-implantation distress. They see how it had represented itself. It is readily recognized and checked. They see how, during the birth it had been believed as actually about to happen, so becoming the basis of a neurotic resistance in adult life. With this complete dossier of information, stretching back to ten days after conception, the subject, who has not been told about this, but has undergone it in the most total way, stage by stage, is now with the clearest of insight, able to recognize where it had created resistances and distorted their behavior, and prevent its happening again.

It is to this kind of integral understanding of the roots of neurotic fixation in adults, that the inclusion of prenatal, first trimester, experience gives us access. It is self-validating to the subject and whoever has worked with him. To the skeptic who says, "It couldn't be", the subject and his companion can only repeat, "Nevertheless that is how it was! Come and experience it, from the inside".

4

Theodicy and the Foetal Experience

Nothing in the discovery of the horrors of the foetal-placental cosmos will have come as a surprise to God. Nor did he wait till we found out about it before he did something to remedy it, indeed all that needed to be done. He accepted responsibility for setting up this sort of human creation, with all its possibilities for foetal contentment, satisfaction and joy, where the mothers of the newly-conceived are loved and tranquil, and where the little person within them is eagerly accepted, recognized and cherished from the moment of a glad and jointly-willed conception. He accepted responsibility also for the possibility of the total absence of this mutual care, plunging the foetus into the hell in which none of these good, reasonable and necessary conditions are available.

What indications do we have of any sensitive planning on God's part as Creator? What evidence is there that he had already taken steps to be able to meet those unfortunate victims, whom his creation would sadistically crush, and not be totally ashamed of himself? Because we must admit he did let it go on, with its inevitable monstrous entail of heart-broken distress to the tiniest of his human creatures, embryos and foetuses, before they are twelve weeks on from their conception. The answer centres in that mysterious yet utterly firm assertion, that God's Son, the sharer of his eternal being and his agent in creation, is also the Lamb of God, slain before the foundation of the world. Redemption is therefore the prior and larger reality, containing creation. It is not so that creation came first and went wrong, requiring redemption as an internal emergency measure.

Charles Williams (1961), in a staggeringly bold essay on the Cross, written in 1943, in the middle of World War II, had this to say:

> The original act of creation can be believed to be good and charitable; it is credible that Almighty God should deign to create beings to

share His joy. It is credible that He should deign to increase their joy by creating them with the power of free will so that their joy should be voluntary. It is certain that if they have the power of choosing joy in Him they must have the power of choosing the opposite of joy in Him. But it is not credible that a finite choice ought to result in an infinite distress; or rather let it be said that, though credible, it is not tolerable (to us) that the Creator should deliberately maintain and sustain his created universe in a state of infinite distress as a result of the choice. (pp. 94-95)

The Origins of Foetal Constriction and Confusion

What is the origin of severe foetal distress? It come about because the foetus is transfused with and imprinted by the mother's own emotions. It is by no means uncommon for the newly-pregnant woman to feel unsupported, surrounded by hostility to herself, on personal grounds in the course of marital accusations, or by her own family. The addition of the baby may mean that housing conditions produce over-crowding, her husband may be unemployed, finances may be tight and managing the necessary expenditures may be a nightmare. The mother-to-be may see no solution, and the foetus within her is imprinted by her feelings of constriction and confusion. The foetus senses that the all-important god-person whose life it shares in all respects, can find no solutions. The foetal conclusion is her conclusion, to survive by such defenses as seem to minimize the damage. That this means keeping people at a distance determined by suspicion of them, for their totally unreasonable refusal to ensure that the most basic, essential, necessary needs of a mother are met. This tends to produce a life-long double stance, expressing her own fundamental rightness and over against it, the world's rigidly maintained injustice, vicious misuse of power and wrongness. She is innocent and good, the world is guilty and bad.

An Indelible Imprinting: Innocent versus Guilty

If this is true for the mother, who may survive into better days, which may give her grounds to revise her polarized, white-versus-black estimate of her cosmos, this is not possible for the foetus. The foetus is indelibly imprinted by these maternal experiences, storing them as they came through at the time and for eternity. It does, in some cases, have enough spare self-hood to protest, in the name of justice and expectation of fairplay, even an expectation that there ought to be love present, against those people and forces it senses are denying the mother her basic rights.

It is the "we" who are innocent and the others who are wicked.

Once gripped by the notion of their total innocence it is not a position from which it is easy, or perhaps even possible, to move. Rather,
there is a regression to this foetal polarization of its own innocence and
the others' guilt, resulting in a paralysis to act in the adult world. The
whole of life is seen through foetal eyes. Though there was in both the
mother and the foetus a total innocence at the time of maximal vulnerability, which is the determined insistence of Job's challenge to his
Creator, there is more to be said to it than that now. They also have
adult memories of culpability, of having made deliberate wrong choices.
Job has no difficulty in agreeing with his moralist accusers, that of course
he is a sinner. But he insists that he must be given freedom to record his
actual experience of life on two quite separate levels which must not be
mixed or run together. On the one he protests his total innocence in the
face of monstrous evil that "came out of the blue" and gratuitously and
wantonly attacked him. On the other he is fully prepared to concede his
sinfulness on the (rather rare it would seem) occasions when he had
been unjust to his neighbours and less than obedient to God.

The Actuality of a Totally Afflicted Identity

A state of infinite, unending distress exists and is maintained in the primal consciousness of all who are victims of the Maternal-Foetal Distress
Syndrome. They can by no means account for it or understand its origins. Yet it is present in them as the first and total experience of their cosmos, kept up in every moment of each day, month, year, for a life-time.
Worthlessness is the result and the designation for the denial of all that
might have made foetal life an ordered mutual exchange of love, moving on into happy personhood. The conviction that "It's not for me" is
based on irrefutable evidence, of being under a kind of curse and a
sense of a dark fate. This is what actually constitutes their basic identity.
There is no disputing the fact, God would have them so. This is "God's
most stern decree".

Questions of Culpability

In an adult world of moral explanations, question of "culpability" and
"guilt" arise, and rightly so, where obedience to God's commands, with
several important exceptions, is reliably held to bring peace and prosper-
ity. This evidently divinely-designed "ditchedness" calls then for some
moral attribution of blame. "Miserable sinner, I must be to blame",

comes spontaneously to the foetal sufferer. Blame and guilt can be handled religiously by penitential ritual, by sorrow for sin, contrition, the proclamation of God's forgiveness and final absolution. The dilemma, for pastoral care that only knows how to proceed on these lines, is that sometimes the most faithful, indeed scrupulous penitent, who moves obediently through all these stages, and has received formal and objective absolution, may feel, in the deepest fiber of his or her nature, not a whit changed. Adult sins have been dealt with, but not this primitive level. The doom bells clang in the depths. This correct penitential transaction in consciousness is evidently quite unheard in these preverbal dungeons.

This realistic model of foetal experience in the first trimester does enable the priest and the penitent, the counsellor and the client, or more commonly, the afflicted person and the afflicted "mate" who has offered to stay with him, in the name of Christ or of an unnamed Christ-like fellow-feeling, to perceive what is going on and to see why the remedies appropriate to conscious, adult, moral transactions, are quite irrelevant here. This model also takes Williams' bold assertion, cited earlier, that it is intolerable to us that the Creator should maintain so many in his creation in a state of infinite distress, presumably for having exercised their free will to choose not to respond to his invitation of shared joy, out of this religious-philosophical frame of reference. Using this frame of reference alone leaves us with a creator so palpably unjust as to be a monster from whom our deepest sense of what is good, fair and just must shrink in contempt and loathing. Our model offers us an alternative frame of reference, in which God can so act as to redeem himself, to justify himself.

The Cross and the Justification of God

This, Charles Williams (1961) perceives, is in some profound and mysterious, more-than-half-hidden sense, God's purpose in the Cross of his Son, Jesus Christ:

> The Cross justifies it to this extent at least, that just as He submitted us to His inexorable will, so He submitted Himself to our wills . . . He made us; He maintained us in our pain. At least, however, on the Christian showing, He consented to be Himself subject to it. If, obscurely, He would not cease to preserve us in the full horror of existence, at least he shared it. This is the first approach to a sense of justice in the whole situation. Whatever He chose, He chose fully, for Himself as for us. This is, I think, unique in theistic religions of the world. I do not

remember any other in which the Creator so accepted his own terms...alone among the gods, He deigned to endure the justice He decreed (pp. 95-96).

This then has seemed to me the most flagrant significance of the Cross; it does enable us to use the word "justice" without shame – which otherwise we could not. God therefore becomes tolerable as well as credible. Our justice condemned the innocent, but the innocent it condemned was one who was fundamentally responsible for the existence of all injustice – its existence in the mere, but necessary, sense of time, which His will created and prolonged. (p. 97)

God as Responsible But Not Victimizer

This maternal-foetal distress model enables us to re-allocate those feelings of being maintained by God, directly and by cruel intention, in infinite distress. We now attribute it to the accident of some of us having been permanently imprinted by our mothers' total distress and rejectedness, and that this inevitably came to have, by the reverberating circuits of memory, the quality of permanence and infinity. In one sense we can take God "off the hook". But in another sense, it is evident that God accepted the inevitability, since the human organism has always dealt with primal pain and catastrophe by repression, in which most of the significant contextual connections of the original experience were lost without a trace. In consequence, he, not the sins of the father for generations impinging on a pregnant mother, would be held to blame. So he accepted the blame, as the Creator in whose world, not only the effects of loving obedience would be carried down in families, blessing the progeny to the fourth generation, but the opposite. Great-grandchildren would suffer from the misguided or wicked choices of eight great-grandparents they had never known. They would be the inheritors of a burden of hateful tendencies, either diminished or potentiated by the intervening generations. The Cross is God's acceptance of the whole attribution of blame to himself, including the blame for the searing effects of maternal distress on foetal persons which leads to all the life-long manifestations of the afflicted "non-person".

God's Response is Remedial, Not Diagnostic

God saw that mere diagnosis, mere retrieval of the actual context of the primal anguish, so as to clarify the causal factors and set the record straight and discharge himself at the bar of his own court of justice, could never be the remedy, could never effect reconciliation. Diagnosis alone cannot so transform afflicted foetal persons as to make them as open to the exchanges of love again as a newly-arrived embryo. God would have to go into the depth of the experience himself, and then arrange for the afflicted, in a most intimate way, to become part of his own body.

The Meaning of the Total Innocence of Christ

I have a growing conviction, strengthened by Sebastian Moore's *The Crucified Jesus is No Stranger* (1977) and now by Rowan William's *Resurrection* (1982), that one of the central dynamic functions of the spotless innocence of Christ, the Lamb of God, who had no culpable sin to repent of, is to make it possible for the millions of people who are paralyzed in the conviction of their own innocence and everybody else's badness, from which no growth or moral progress is possible, to encounter Christ at that foetal depth, while recognizing its original context, and emerge from the trap with the help of Christ's total innocence. His non-blaming assistance in the work of the retrieval of memory brings many things to mind that bring truthfulness to the record, a corrective humility and a realistic penitence. The protest of being the victim, the innocent persecuted one at the time of honest-openness and total vulnerability, is in no way denied. It is affirmed, and Christ comes alongside in his innocent affliction, to share and help in the bearing of those foetal horrors. The protest is given a voice and is fully validated.

Once this basic protest of innocent victimization has been heard and put in a context felt and reliably recognized as the correct one, the pressure to go on insisting on this polarized view of life disappears. The primal view, which in all integrity had to insist on its accuracy, has been validated. There is therefore no longer any need to go on insisting on it. The paralyzing, self-limiting foetal agenda completed, the regressed Christian can emerge from the death in which it had encapsulated him, and begin to respond as an adult to the precious gifts that surround him in a fellowship sustained by the Word of God, the Sacrament of the Lord's betrayed-while-innocent Body, and the Fellowship of those who live by the same death and resurrection realities.

Memory can then go on retrieving what memory does, many occasions on which we are called upon to face our own past sinfulness. Not that this leads to penitential self-flagellation. Not at all. It is under-taken with Christ, whose intention, like that of the Prodigal's father, is never to chide or remonstrate, or create conditions of acceptance in which self-esteem would be threatened (that is the moralistic elder brother's style), but always to welcome the returning sinner who has "come to himself" and decided to risk going back home.

Self-judgment and self-condemnation are damaging, not only because of my cruel alienation and rejection of the victim, but because the adoption of the judgmental attitude diminishes me. I am killing off part of myself. The generous, caring self, in the power of God reaching out to the wretched self to draw it into compassionate closeness, is strangled by hostility and rejection. The oppressive and condemnatory role wounds and diminishes me. I become the victim of my own destructiveness whenever I split myself into a condemnatory part which is prepared to kill off my own impulse to loving-kindness and mercifulness. That killed-off part becomes the victim who is "crucified with Christ". The murderer will have to remember that murder of the innocent blood and confess to being also the "crucifier of Christ". Both are aspects of me. It is vital that I recognize that Christ relates to both of these in his saving love. The murderer and the victim are both his beloved. But I am not allowed to forget that I am the murderer.

A New Heredity in a New Creation

These foetal sufferers' heredity in the natural order of creation had gone so wretchedly wrong that arrangements would have to be made for them to be conceived again, within this new divine initiative, and provided with a new heredity. This heredity would be derived, by God's loving contrivance, entirely from the Son, who took upon him our human flesh, and in it suffered, was afflicted and died cruelly, and was then, by his Father, raised to totally victorious life, in all of which we would be invited to share. So the natural heredity and its disastrous origin and outcome would be lovingly penetrated. Its sufferings would be re-lived and felt again, but this time with none of the original bewilderment as to probable personal worthlessness and completely free of the suspicion of blame. This penetration would be effected by the totally accepting and sharing love of Christ, the author and perfector of the new covenant of unbreakable love, and he is quite undaunted by all our life-long denials of this new and saving relationship.

This has been the pattern of my experience of him, acting in this way with me, in the fifty years of my conscious life as a Christian, and no doubt it extends back in the same pattern a further eighteen years to my conception. It would be especially true from my baptism when I was objectively joined to this second heredity, by the loving grace of God.

The Denial of Evil and the Loss of Memory

There is consequently no point now in attempting to deny, as the conventionally religious habitually do, that there is a mass of evil in the world, of destructiveness in the most intimate relationships in families and social groups, including our own, even if we are "Christians". The net religious effect of trying to live up to "being a Christian" of the conventional sort is not to have less destructiveness and self-seeking at the expense of others rooting about in their lives. It is simply to have to spend more effort in denying it, not just hiding it from others who would be conventionally shocked by it, but hiding it also from themselves. They have lost a true memory of the facts and have become incorrigible.

They do their utmost to obliterate the memory of their serious sins and shortcomings. Being prepared to chatter about the trivial ones is no threat; it gives an impression of a devoutly developed faculty of self-criticism, insight and readiness to remember and acknowledge one's failings. It actually builds up the false-self system of the religious need for success in conventional living. "Religious" here, must be extended to include all the conventionally moral, decent people, who have ideals and "try to be good".

The deep memories, of real significance to their relationship to their dark and negative side, they suppress and reject. Yet it is in these deep places that they still reject and alienate the weak self in themselves, despise the self who was driven to despair, yell at the one who got anxious to shut up, crush and kick downstairs the quite justifiably enraged child of the past. They dally with the sexy self, in fantasy indulging it for a while and then with prudish fervour, look the other way. They gloat over the torture they devise for those they envy or are jealous of, and then get ready to be nice to them. All these real memories they struggle to suppress, for they have no intention, any more than their religious group has, of ever forgiving or being reconciled to these weak and despised selves, or ever conceiving that they could be admitted as acceptable members of a community of the once disreputable and despised, such as Jesus always creates.

Anamnesis

So the way back to Christ, to inner integrity and to membership of the forgiven, reconciled, responsible, open and fully sharing Body of Christ, the return to the community, must be through the recovery of memory. Rowan Williams (1982) formulates this very vigorously in his penetratingly clear and accurate study of what the resurrection must mean for Christians, when it is allowed to mean what it intrinsically does, and is not denied by our fantasies and idolatries about what God ought and ought not to keep alive.

> There is no healing of the memory until the memory itself is exposed as a wound, a loss. Yet this must equally happen without its reappearing as a threat . . . The word of forgiveness is not audible for the one who has not "turned" to his or her past, and the degree to which an unreal or neutralized memory has come to dominate is the degree to which forgiveness is difficult. (p. 21)

Williams writes of memory and the need for its recovery if Christian communities are to become true to Christ's "acceptance of the unacceptable". There is thus the need for the anamnesis (or not forgetting) which must track down the memories of childhood, and, if there be any relevant memories earlier than that, even from the womb, then to those also. It is unusual for a theologian to press for this essentially psychotherapeutic approach. He writes:

> When we diminish or victimize ourselves in our violence to others, we are part responding to the incomprehensible and buried memory of "diminutions" experienced in the pre- and semi-conscious state of our earliest years – or months or days. Even in the most loving of parent-child relations, unconscious and unintended violence can occur; and it has taken a very long time for the realization to dawn that the experience of birth itself may be the primary and traumatic deprivation, "robbery with violence"...if the relations of human beings have in them an irreducible element of mutual diminution or deprivation, "violent" displacement or exclusion, we can understand that fundamental and pervasive lack in the human world of a sense of being affirmed, accepted, given a place, given a share, which generate the impulse towards the self-protective, self-affirming exclusion and diminution of others. It has been said that Jesus was betrayed in "the lost childhood of Judas". George Bernanos could write boldly of Hitler as an *enfant humilie*, responding with pathological intensity and on an enormous scale to a profound experience (in no way understood, faced, or assimilated) of deprivation.
>
> By discovering my past of oppression, I can discover my own self-diminution in the process; and in pressing back to the source of this vicious spiral, I discover the primary lack of wholeness, the primary deprivation, which is part of belonging to the single human story. (pp. 24-25)

The Absence of Affirmation

When Rowan Williams (1982) writes of a "fundamental lack in the human world of a sense of being affirmed, accepted, given a place, given a share" (p. 24), the whole of my experience of listening to what people say when they are virtually reliving the commonest sources of ingrained unhappiness in the early months of life in the womb indicates that this phase of development is predominately the one in which such pervasive feelings take their origin. Of course, the newborn in a neglectful home has reason to feel all these emotions. We find, however, when post-natal troubles are being re-lived, that all kinds of other things are being complained of as irksome, which have more to do with defects in the way "the nursing couple" is functioning. Some adults complain of being unnoticed, their presence totally unrecognized, of being in a place that is there, but which clearly has "no place" for them, of wanting to have some sense of sharing life and interchange of loving give-and-take, but meeting a blank wall of total unresponsiveness, as if all the eager longings were dead letters sent to some dear person who actually lives elsewhere (as Gerard Manley Hopkins' poem "I Wake and Feel the Fell of Dark, Not Day" [1967] has it). When we track down with them the actual context and source of these specific feelings by means of primal integration work, this particular constellation of pervasive feelings is invariably discovered to be the response of the foetus, in the first half of the pregnancy, to a mother who has no inkling of the fact that during those months a foetus is a person waiting to be related to and given what these folk lack. Indeed those mothers who do have an innate sense (undamaged by cultural insensitivity drilled into women by the media, by other women, particularly those who are pro-abortion, and by doctors who could not conceive of foetal personhood) that "I have a person in here with whom it is good and proper to relate in all these ways often in the day", are probably quite uncommon in the community nowadays.

The Road Back

The road back to the formation of a truly Christ-like community is one on which the disreputable, and by the world's social standards, unacceptable (because "unrespectable") aspects of ourselves and others, are called home and made welcome to the table to eat together in friendship. We must see that this Christian maturing is not just a road looking forward in time. It is first of a road that rolls backward, in order to recover devalued but actually precious, if painful memories.

But if we are to foster truly Christian communities, in which we are habitually acting in a Christ-like way towards the once hated and rejected aspects of ourselves and others which have been rejected, not because Christ rejects them, quite the contrary, he loves them, but because the self-image of respectable and religious people cannot include such disgraceful doings and feelings as a true part of them, the only way back to truth and integrity from this falsehood must be through the opening up of personal memories. All the force of religious habit will resist this. It will be called morbid. We will be told that St. Paul says "I don't look back, I press forward" (Philippians 3:13). The time spent on this return journey to the recovery of personal memories, in which many lost emotions will be retrieved and expressed for the first time, and given a voice, and not cut short but encouraged to find full expression, will be disapprovingly called time misspent in emotional self-indulgence. We will be asked whether, in a world in which so many concrete tasks have to be done, this isn't a selfish waste of precious time. If you answer that St. Paul said to Timothy, "Attend to yourself and to the teaching" (I Timothy 4:16) and that you are following the same priority, it will cut no ice. If those who take this road of the uncovering of personal memory are still in contact with those who favour the old way, which they almost certainly will, it is well to be forewarned of their objections.

The Presence of Christ

The recovery-of-guilty-memory road essentially arises out of being with the risen Jesus, meeting him as the disciples did in Galilee or back in Jerusalem, after his resurrection. They had been with him in the weeks leading up to his crucifixion. He had told them he was to suffer and they had persistently changed the subject. The leaders, those near the top of the heap, had taken group time to argue about who was to have the chief seats in the coming kingdom. When they met Jesus, after the suffering he had been trying to tell them about had been fully endured, they had to face the memory of the crass stupidity and irrelevance of the talk about "who should be first" that had so engaged their attention then. There was no way back into fellowship with the risen Jesus now, except by jogging their memory of these shameful facts, accepting that they were sinful and stupid men. They had actually done these things. It would be no good to say, "Lord, if I show that I am very sorry, and punish myself for being bad, will you wipe the negative score card clean, and let it be as though it had never happened?" That is a religious ploy which is determined to expunge the memory and give oneself a "clean start", so that one never actually accepts responsibility for having been seduced by sinful attitudes and having made bad choices. It is to prefer a split self, full of denials and condemned to life-long immaturity.

The alternative, in the presence of Jesus to accept fully the responsibility for saying, "This is the kind of man I am", does not lead to any penitential rigmarole. Why not? Because Jesus does not require any, nor do the others in whom the same process of integration of "reality-about-myself" is going on. The only work Christ required of them was the honest rolling back of memory to acknowledge the facts, not complimentary ones but true ones, about themselves. Then, in the presence of Christ, as they looked into his eyes they would see, not reproach, or any sort of blame, for, after all "he knew what was in men" and he had known exactly what would happen and told them so beforehand. In his presence, they saw his recognition of what they were and that was the end of the matter.

Subjects often speak of this strong sense of Christ's presence with them during some particularly agonizing exposure of foetal distress, as when realizing that the mother, who is "God in this foetal cosmos", had no intention at all of recognizing, much less welcoming, their presence. The same may arise during foetal attempts to deal with the inescapable need to know from "the Beloved" (for that the mother still is), that they exist and that their existence is recognized and accepted. Without this, a total sense of worthlessness and a most radical sense of guilt descend. The guilt may be that, "I ought never to have appeared in your life and asked for a place in it", or that "In some inexplicable way I am not able to be what you would require for 'acceptance'". This is not moral guilt, guilt that I have done wrong, but "ontological" guilt, guilt that I exist at all. Nothing can be done about it.

The presence of Christ alongside, welcoming, a beloved presence, valuing the worthless, insisting on making a place where there is secure belonging, dissolving the "guilt" in the warmth of reassurance, rests, reconciles and satisfies the vulnerable foetal person. This may happen without reference to Christ himself, the same transformations happening with the person of the facilitator, who is fully open and totally attentive, and able to be the catalyst, and more, the mediator of these precious reconciliations.

5

Transmarginal Mechanisms and
The Roots of Affliction

The world of fourth level transmarginal stress is mechanism dominated. Indeed, this was one of the puzzles when we had thought most of this took place in the post-natal phase when there are people around the afflicted baby, however cluelessly and inhumanely they behave. So when we read, in Simone Weil (1961):

> If the mechanism were not blind, there would not be any affliction. Affliction is anonymous before all things. It deprives its victims of their personality and makes them into things. It is indifferent; and it is the coldness of this indifference – a metallic coldness – which freezes all those it touches right to the depths of their souls. They will never find warmth again. They will never believe any more that they are anyone (p. 125).

We begin to see that we do not need to try to account for this as a post-natal happening. It sounds very much like what adults report as the foetal experience of becoming aware of existing in an ice-cold, silent because totally uncherished, womb. Again Simone Weil wrote:

> Affliction . . . is a simple and ingenious device which introduces into the soul of a finite creature the immensity of force, blind, brutal and cold. The infinite distance which separates God from the creature is entirely concentrated into one point to pierce the soul in its centre....The man to whom such a thing happens has no part in the operation. He struggles like a butterfly which is pinned alive into an album. (p. 135)

The recognition that arises out of findings from the first trimester experiences of the foetus is immediate. This is what Simone Weil was reaching down to within herself. We do not need to struggle to interpret it in post-natal terms, or even as birth where the suffering is impersonal, brutal, mechanical, and blind, but is remembered as skull-splitting pressure on the head, whereas this supra-maximal distress is focused on the navel and transfixed belly. The Maternal-Foetal Distress Syndrome, in one or several of its many variants, affecting every part of the body, surfaces to provide the content of the afflicted person's communication with whoever is alongside him or her in mutual care.

Somatic Displacement

This foetal rejection-displacement-containment defensive system proves to be the origin of the body "blocks" at different levels, described in detail and worked on by Alex Lowen and his associates in *Bioenergetics* (1976). While re-living the first trimester, the adult becomes aware that as a foetus it was trying to push the badness into the legs and feet. One priest whose feet were so badly distorted with chronic muscular tension as to be advised that a surgical operation was needed, began to recognize the primal source of it. He decided to intensify and discharge it, which he did with some symptomatic relief. Once would not be enough for the resolution of that syndrome. Others find masochistic pleasure in attacking the skin of the soles of the feet, and may realize where it started. One young man with severe recurrent arthritis of the knees recognized the mode by which he had attempted to survive as a foetus, locking the intense "badness" in the knees. When I suggested "re-owning" the "misused" knees, saying "Can you become your right knee", he turned violent and profane. "I hate the bloody thing. I don't want anything to do with it". Later, he became sufficiently strong to do some identifying with the scapegoated knee, with considerable symptomatic relief.

In other cases the "umbilical badness" is displaced into the thighs, men despising their musculature and women convinced that their thighs, which feel sore and heavy, are fat, ugly and so unsightly they will not bathe, while objectively there is nothing at all unshapely about them.

Blocks at the pelvic brim consign the reproductive organs to all the negative feelings appropriate to the invasive "filth" from the mother's distressed world. Dysmenorrhea is a common expression of this, as is the compulsive need to focus distrust, refusal and repugnance upon what should normally be pleasurable sexual intimacy and intercourse. The foetus of the next generation, fated to come to conscious awareness in this cold hell is always horribly distressed to find itself embedded in this inhuman frigidity. Always feeling cold, the emotional paralysis of coming from frozen wastes, pursues such unfortunates into adult life. Or if she regards the whole site with aversion, as despicable, it is a correspondingly repulsive place for the foetus. Recognition and courageous re-living can change the whole picture.

The level of the diaphragm is an obvious barrier below which to attempt to restrain the evil influx. This often results in the perpetuation of the original non-displaced sensations of the foetus during the primal onslaught. A quite agonizing pain may be felt at the navel, like a penetrating nail, felt as rough or rusty, or a spear-thrust or a succession of arrows. Commonly the invasive "stuff" is felt as black, "gooey", nauseating, shitty, bitter, hard and lumpy, and so damaging to the vulnerable foetal organism as to be poisonous. We realize that we understand for the first time the specific metaphors and images of Job's lament:

> I am a mark for his archery, his arrows are all about me; still they pierce me to the marrow, drain my life, pour out my bowels on the ground; wound upon wound, giant hands assail me (Job 16:12-13).

> The Almighty has buried his arrow deep in me. His poison drinks up my spirit as I drink it up. All his terrors set themselves in array against me (Job 6:4).

Negative umbilical affect is commonly displaced into the skin, giving rise to infantile eczema and recurrent atopic dermatitis. Job seems to have suffered severely with this, with the added complication of flies and maggots. There may actually break out, as we re-live this assault, a local inflammation round the area of the navel itself.

A knotted tension in the region of the solar plexus, from which relief is impossible to obtain, is felt both during the first-trimester re-living and as a predominant life complaint. Thereafter, children who become known as "little belly achers" suffer persistently from it. The whole concept of hypochondriasis, of pain and fearful apprehension of impending fatal disease, located "below the rib-cage" is now firmly allocated, as to its origins, to this early intra-uterine distress, funneled in from distresses in the maternal world.

If the diaphragmatic barrier is overwhelmed by the invading badness, it is symbolically experienced as filling the chest, with a last ditch defense at the base of the neck. I have already mentioned what happens when the only safe, good place has become the brain. Intellectual activities are the only ones that one can rely on as one's own, guarded rigorously against the destructiveness all around. We find this to be one of the main sources of those dynamic defenses which characterize the schizoid, intellectual, introverted, in every way gnostic personality defenses.

Differentiation

Again, we begin to see why a premature, forced and utterly unnatural "differentiation", between itself and the mothering womb, queers the whole pitch for all subsequent differentiations. It has become itself a dirty word, synonymous with the need for the most agonizing splitting. In one sense, to have effected this primal splitting or differentiation into opposition to the mother was life saving. But to have, as one's basic cosmos, one's world-with-God, a place of such soul-destroying intentions as to require such evasive action, is to have a good reason, when you have found a moderately satisfactory definitive niche, not to budge out of it into growth and development, for these imply a trustable and non-persecutory universe.

The Syndrome of Affliction

From the knowledge we now have of foetal existence early in the womb, this devastating sense of having been fated with a totally negative, non-human identity is at last explicable. We can understand how it came to be so, and under those maternal circumstances, could not otherwise than be so. Our understanding of the active dynamic dissociation of the total original event, achieved by repression, enables us to comprehend how the horrific force of the experience itself can, in some people, never be repressed. In others, it can break out from repression during some childhood, adolescent or adult crisis of miserable failure or rejection, and refuse to be repressed again. In yet other, more "normal" citizens, it constitutes that nucleus of inner fear from which their whole lives, in every urgent ploy, are in flight: "That must never be me."

Murderous Splitting

Our experience of spending thousands of hours with those who are reliving the effects of maternal-foetal distress in the first trimester gives us significant evidence of the nature of this splitting. It is a mechanism that compels the victim coping with maximal pain to realize that it is driven into the endurance of even more intolerable pain if it continues to identify with the hopeful, still expectant, life-oriented foetal self. To turn away from it savagely and to kill it off is to reduce the pain of pursuing what is evidently a vain hope. The foetal self, tempted to kill something to reduce the pain, picks on the stupidly hopeful self. So the foetal self, tempted to murder, sensing that it only increases the pain unnecessarily if it does not dis-identify with the fatuously hopeful self, symbolically does the deed. Consequently the murder, the victimization of the persistently life-oriented, good self, feels entirely justifiable. We have met this complex foetal "reasoning" on a sufficient number of occasions to warrant our offering this interpretation.

Our adult victimization and rejection of others, who present themselves as wretched victims, hanging on to life in the face of all the evidence that they would be better dead, arouses in us the same split-off ambivalence as the first trimester "solution", which transmarginal stress set up in us. Now we act destructively towards them, to save ourselves from the added pain, which we are sure would come to us if we took back the intolerable burden of being alive and responsive to their, or our, wretched weakness and worthlessness.

Compressing the record of hundreds of those who have made the prenatal journey, it is apparent that if the distress is within the bounds of coping, the foetus often takes the attack of retributive resentment totally to itself, sparing the mother. But transmarginal, supra-maximal foetal distress is another matter. It ceases to be a matter of choice. Mechanisms, of the kind brilliantly described by "catastrophe theory", take over. There simply is no choice in the matter. Pain beyond a certain intensity causes splitting. The part determined to survive by reducing the pain, dissociates itself from the weak, pathetic, evidently contemptible and worthless self, which the cosmos evidently does not think worth stirring itself to answer, and hates it with the callousness that belongs to the "cosmic sadist". There is no sense of meaning, therefore, in attributing any blame to the foetus for having become an involuntary murderer of its own resolutely hopeful self. The theodicy of Julian of Norwich plumbs these depths, and her constant theme, as she stays with them and Christ together is, "I saw no blame" (1966).

Foetal Deprivation

Rosemary Haughton, in *The Passionate God* (1981), remarks that "children deprived of love cannot value or love themselves, and until someone else does they are 'empty' and warped in their whole growth" (p. 93). What we are now compelled to realize is that this deprivation of recognition, caring and respectful attention, acceptance, and in short, love, which leads to the most total sense of worthlessness, is typically an experience of the foetal person in the first trimester. If that is the case, what is meant by the remedial response, "Until someone else loves them they remain empty and warped in their whole growth"? While both the deprivation and the remedial loving were portrayed in psychodynamics as post-natal mother-baby interactions, the "exchange of love" was all fairly comprehensible and much closer to adult interchange of love than this foetal deprivation. Our new perspective takes the whole task into a different sphere, a sphere we had barely known existed, but one to which it will become increasingly important to be able to return, both with human and Christ-like love and sharing. Until we can help the foetal self to understand and be reconciled to its very proper and inevitable refusals of "the other" in the prenatal sphere, there is no reason to expect, on the part of the foetal self, a willingness to accept the transition of birth into the post-natal sphere where it is invited to give a loving response of acceptance to the same mother.

So, when Rowan Williams puts on record these feelings as quite pervasive and "a fundamental lack in the human world", knowing as we do where they take their origin, one can only ask, "How could it be otherwise?" It will remain so for as long as pregnant women behave in this way. It will be remedied, and cease to be the pervasive bane it now is, exactly insofar as pregnant women re-learn the old wisdom, devoting the time of pregnancy, not to topping up the hire-purchase funds by working overtime, but to the intimate tender care of the person growing within the womb, and of her own tranquility and settledness within her own inner and outer worlds.

The Ideal Paradigm of Early Pregnancy

The paradigm of this tender care can be observed in the Blessed Mother Mary's actions following her visit from the angel. There is, from the viewpoint of the first trimester development and its crucial importance, far exceeding that of subsequent months, an exact appropriateness in the movements and provisions which the Blessed Mother Mary makes for herself and the developing foetus within her. As soon as the Annunciation is over, she shares with the Spirit what she should do. Wait and tell Joseph the impossible news that he is the first man in universal history to have a betrothed who is pregnant, but not by him or another man? This is hardly a sensible option. Nazareth is no place for her just now. Elizabeth? Yes. She, too, is having a child by divine appointment, long past child-bearing years, who is to be the herald of a far greater Coming One. So Mary "rose up in haste", and hurried down to the hill country of Judea to spend three months with Elizabeth. The greeting of the agile John, leaping in Elizabeth's womb as Mary enters, confirmed the arrangement. So the two godly and wise women are left in peace and to their prayers, totally open to God, who had more to do with what was growing in their wombs than any men-folk. They did not even have a talkative priest about the house, since Zechariah had been rendered dumb.

At the end of an ideal "first trimester" for Mary, totally supportive for both the women who had been able to give each other mutual help at the deepest possible level, and ideal for Jesus, who by this arrangement, was ensured the most perfect possible time of sharing with his "lovely and beautiful" mother, the Beloved to whom his foetal yearning reached out and by whom he was totally satisfied, the difficult future could be met. Mary then felt safe, and rightly so, to face the very tricky situation back in Nazareth with Joseph.

Now, with the baby three months on the way, it was no longer possible to hide the fact of an apparently illegitimate pregnancy. At first, Joseph was minded to divorce Mary quietly, not wanting a scandal, or the punishment that lurked by law in the background for such women, death by stoning. As she walked up the hill to Nazareth, Mary would be spiritually well-prepared for the inevitable crisis. This event could not go wrong. Somehow, God would get through to Joseph, as indeed He did.

We have listened to and recorded dozens of instances where the relationship of mother and foetus is basically good and mutually supportive, when the foetus has responded to temporary trouble and crisis in the mother's world by a clear sense of being eager and able to support her. Its own sense of security is, by this stage, quite well-enough established to enable it to form the intention of supporting the mother, wanting her to be free of any charge on her attention on its account. There is no reason to believe that, by the beginning of the fourth month, and even much earlier, this would not be the case with Jesus. So the whole episode of the return to Nazareth and the period of Joseph's hesitation would be a positive and constructive experience of sharing, and of rising to the responsibility created by the months of total maternal availability.

The Modern Situation

It is difficult for us, living in Western Europe or the North American continent towards the end of the 20th century, to conceive of what it would be like to live in a culture that gave the very highest priority to preserving maternal tranquility. We don't know what it is like to live in a socie-ty that gave the foetus, the human citizen of the next generation, the best possible conditions to develop as an emotionally, physically and spiritually healthy person. Yet we are told that in the ancient stable cul-tures of China two thousand years ago, this was the norm. When a woman became pregnant, a family conference would be held, extend-ing if need be beyond the family, to ensure that all burdens and such involvements as might disturb her tranquility were removed. Others shared more of the ordinary strains of living so that she could be relieved of them and devote herself to providing a peaceful womb for the foetus. My Chinese friends in Singapore have assured me that this ideal is far from forgotten, even though the inroads of Western culture have made it more difficult to achieve. Indeed, it has been called into question by those who are being seduced by Western ways.

In India, the custom of the woman's returning home to her mother, and away from the mother-in-law's influence, which, in traditional lore, seldom makes for tranquility, as the young bride's husband is totally under his mother's thumb and cannot protect her, is intended to reach the same purpose. It has the disadvantage in that her life with her hus-band is disrupted. Not that that is encouraged to grow to the point where endearments are shown in front of the family. Traditionally, any emotional expression must be clandestine. In this sense, perhaps Western ways have brought some healthy freedoms to the minority who are free to adopt them. But educated Indian Christian women make a priority of the continuance of their professional working lives. Children early become the responsibility of ayahs. They would find it hard to be asked to make adjustments to improve the emotional health back-ground of their foetuses in the first trimester!

When we turn to the Jewish people through the millennia, we detect a deep respect, care and protection of the mother in the centre of the household. Marriages were, and still are, carefully arranged. By seven-teen years old the girl would have been betrothed and married. The bar mitzvah training, which her husband would have completed at the age of fourteen, provided him with a clear and specific account of how he should behave towards his young wife. Inexperience was compensated for by training based on the wisdom of the ages. He was not to go to the wars since this would introduce anxiety. Of course, national disasters would disturb this essentially tranquil norm, but even here, the protec-tion of the womenfolk was a priority.

In such a theocratic culture as the Hebrew one, in which most preg-nant women would be able to offer optimal conditions for foetal development from conception to birth, almost all the babies born would have had excellent opportunities to prosper in every way during the most crucial months of development. They would grow up into adults undamaged by a load of neurotic projections. Indeed, for the most part, they would not only be able, as adults, to see life with undistorted perceptions, they would have that reservoir of courage and optimism which wells up into life at times of crisis.

All this to say that, in times past, the "Ideal" was perhaps even the achieved norm, including as we have seen, elements of constructive and happy "Coping". But to be driven into desperate "Opposition" and to get fixated there would be uncommon. "Transmarginal stress" would be so rare that in the whole Old Testament, Job is the only unmistakable sufferer, though other desperate, self-destructive characters like King Saul, could be among them, as Thomas was among the disciples.

The West's Terrible Reversal

Nowadays, the situation for pregnant mothers in Western society is such that the "Ideal" may even have become rare. Being stressed has become the norm, with which the majority of foetuses, the next generation of children, of adolescents, of young married couples or those who remain single, of middle-aged and aged, will have to contend. It is a terrifying thought and a cataclysmic prospect, yet no observer of the social scene, with all its rising indices of disruption and fragmentation, can seriously doubt that it is upon us.

The Imperative of Remedial Action

A considerable proportion of the weight of these research findings is to point to one of the root causes, among many contributory ones, as being the appalling decline in the standards of care and self-care of pregnant women, particularly in the distressing uncertainties of the first trimester. By the same logic, the only way forward is to reverse this, in every way pressing upon all those who will listen, the vital importance, for the emotional health and survival of the next generation, of beginning to provide them with tranquil mothers.

6

Wisdom and Counselling

Education is not simply a matter of "drawing people out" so that they discover themselves. The educator has been educated. That means that he has learned to draw out certain things that he or his teachers believes to be important. Important for what, we may ask? The important should be the general principles of a subject, allowing the student to "see the wood for the trees". So that when faced by a lot of detailed input, he can sort it out and know how to act so that the main issues are dealt with and the subsidiary ones put aside.

But however small or large a "chunk of life" we are considering, this choice of what is and what isn't "important" is always bound to be a matter of opinion. Further, opinions shared by one group of educators (or put forward by an "opinionated" one) become "theories". The theories that take root over the years become assumptions. We are presently going through a time when the basic assumptions about what education is, or ought to be, is being radically questioned.

The work of counselling rests on the education of some to help others in times of distress. It inevitably has as its aim that of equipping us with the ability to perceive, within the confusion, what the main underlying causes are, and those contradictory ones which have to be dealt with in order to bring relief.

What Has Happened to the Wise?

From the beginning of the history of communal men this has been the task of wise men and wise women. Wisdom has been the faculty of discernment which could penetrate the disguises human beings throw over their motives and subtle actions until they have mixed themselves up thoroughly. The wise could see through to the truth that had to be faced and the actions, by that person or others, which needed to be taken. What has happened to wisdom? Are there no wise persons among us, or have our assumptions changed so that we do not respect them any longer? The proliferation of professional training schemes to make one "wise", with qualifications and accreditations to prove it, has displaced, in the esteem of intellectual circles, if not among the common folk, the honour that used to come to the wise. The honour came not by examination, but by a gradually growing recognition that here was a person endowed with gifts of wisdom and thus responsible in exercising them. Age increased this capacity. The wise were not retired at sixty-five on a pension.

Displacement of Home-Grown Wisdom by Professional Training

We have done this as a culture but are becoming disillusioned by the performance, even within their own fields, of the most highly trained persons, professionally "wise" in handling difficult human problems. Psychiatrists would insist that their training and expertise is in the field of mental illness and psychopathological disorders. They have neither the desire nor the training to take on the people's emotional muddles, craziness and stubbornness. This, they affirm, is a role that has been foisted on them, and with even greater unreasonable pressure (because of direct and unselected access) upon general practitioners. None of these physicians would claim that their specialist knowledge of diseases adds up to wisdom about the "chief end of man", as to what human nature essentially is, and how it is meant by its "designer" to work. Sensitive psychiatrists are troubled that they often have nothing better to offer than drugs. In the short term, the use of drugs for the relief of overwhelming anxiety is a great blessing. In the long-term, used as a suppressant over many years, the result often looks like a curse. Yet within psychiatry itself, the criteria to call a halt, and ask whether more is not being lost than gained, and insist on research to find alternatives, are lacking. Since these would certainly involve the whole community in a great deal more costly caring, and for this they are unwilling, the medical profession is left with the thankless task of keeping the miserable quiet.

In psychoanalysis, theory has taken over, and thus a method that is reassuring and in various ways rewarding to those who practice it. Careful, and not unsympathetic, observers of the psychoanalytic scene are troubled. The gradual conversion of self-determining persons into indoctrinated, stereotyped and often chronically dependent patients has overshot the point of benefit by some years. Again, within psychoanalysis itself, the criteria which would demand that the analyst cry halt, ask these fundamentally human questions, break off and seek other approaches, are apparently lacking. Furthermore, in spite of the very high value the various analytic schools place on the accuracy of their particular theories and interpretations, the evidence has not been encouraging. Rigorous studies of actual effectiveness do not show any of their theories to be superior over any other, or even relevant to therapeutic outcomes. Orthodox Freudians, like many other therapists, both benefit and make worse their patients, or may have no appreciable effect on them.

How much wisdom has come of extending the calls made on psychiatrists and general practitioners, giving them a public mandate to be in charge not only of the genuinely mentally ill, but of marital problems and social stresses of all kinds, on behalf of all of us in society, is very doubtful. Many doctors firmly decline to discuss non-medical matters. Yet the spill-over from inter-personal and intra-personal stress into psychosomatic illness, makes this difficult to maintain. Those who do open up on the emotional issues and their causes find it hard to know where to stop. Since they know that society offers the patients no one else to turn to, out of compassion and a genuine interest in people, they act way beyond the doctor's remit and permit society to go on fudging the issue.

Counsellors and Boundaries

The training of counsellors and their appointment to work in various settings and with various populations, such as pastoral, marital, family, adolescent, middle and old age, and for various problems, such as addictions, psychosexual problems, financial issues, intractable behavior, and character problems, is thus critically important. Supervision, vital to the ongoing maintenance of sound boundary functioning, must be an integral part of the process. Counsellors must offer genuine and deep caring while being watchful for occasions when the counsellor gets hooked into the counsellee's fantasy that "you have made yourself responsible for being, twenty-four hours a day, as attentive as my parent ought to have been". That is nonsense, yet I have supervised dozens of clergy and social worker counsellors for whom it had become the prime obligation of their existence. To break it they have had to bear the "guilt of being made to feel cruel and faithless". But this has become a power game, in which they have handed over all their personal power to the counsellee's voracious fantasies. It is, however, crueler to let it continue. The regressed "child" in the counsellee will not give up this malignant power without a fight, but until they do, the "disease" gets worse, potentiating itself. Healing, which begins with the taking of responsibility for being, not a "child", but an "adult" accepting reasonable help without power-games, cannot take its first steps. This gift, of deeply caring while wisely maintaining boundaries, is the kind of enabling which the counselling profession brings to the national health scene, together with the patience and ability to maintain it, untiring because never over-tired, if necessary over the course of months and years.

The Training of Counsellors

Not burdened with the need to justify their existence as a school of the specially expert by demonstrating the correctness of Freud's (or any other) theory, counsellors can stay much closer to their clients, using empathy to live within their world and see life through their eyes. This is at least one stage closer to true wisdom, because it begins by embracing the distressed person's chaos of turbulent feeling, respecting them and being genuinely available to them. Counsellors create some professional distance and limit their time commitment to interviews, at times prolonged, but the wide emotional distance usually observed between "the real experts", the psychiatrists and the analysts and their patients, is not erected.

Dependence on Rogerian Theory and Practice

Carl Rogers has been a central figure in developing the discipline of counselling. The widespread training of ministers as pastoral counsellors has been mostly based on Rogerian principles of counselling. Rogers himself had been a theological student. In protest at the insensitive way religion stood in critical judgment over those who had suffered breakdowns, blaming them for failure in religious performance, he broke with religion. So did St. Paul, but he had the corrective wisdom of the good news of the gracious action of God the Father, in Christ's unconditional acceptance of the broken, to take its place. Rogers offered his own "unconditional acceptance". He intended to be "client-centered" and "non-directive" and these have become the aims of the world-wide counselling training movement. "Client-centeredness" is saying that the wisdom to comprehend and solve your problem is within you. There is much that is wise about this assertion, because a large part of the truth is there, but overlaid, neglected, feared, and scorned in the name of popular cultural assumptions. Perhaps the commonest of these rejected truths to emerge on reflection in counselling, unless the counsellor is hostile to such ideas, is the realization that, "I have been determined to go it alone, without help from man or God, and that just isn't possible. It isn't in human nature to do it. It has been a crazy project, doomed to failure. Where do I turn now?"

Rogerian Group Therapy

Rogers had his answer in group therapy. "Meet with others, let intimacy and deep mutual inter-dependence grow. Discover yourself in deepening sharing, openness, honesty, caring and sustaining. My non-directiveness has directed you to this richly human activity. Beyond that there is no 'revealed' wisdom to direct you to. Particularly I do not push at you the beliefs and opinions of any church denomination about God and what He requires of you. My humanist groups will protect you from that kind of burdensome imposition, for we all agree about religion. It is irrelevant to personal growth and personality change and more likely to fossilize you than bring you to personal fulfillment."

Regrettably, as things are in the Churches, and in the personality interactions within the most "aggressive" evangelistic agencies, there is wisdom in Rogers' assumptions. People should be protected, not from the message of the church as such, but from the "cultural package" that often has to be accepted with it, under threat of being rejected again.

"God-talk" Discouraged

The result is that most counselling agencies, even including those which have been established by Christians or by churches, are firm in directing their counsellors not to introduce "God talk". Even if the client introduces it, it is quite probably part of a strategy to avoid emotional issues the client does not want to grapple with. That may be true as well. But is the need for a loving relationship with God ever raised in counselling in a fully authentic way? And what does the counsellor do then?

That depends entirely on his or her own state of faith and commitment to Christ. The stronger that is, the more he will have wanted to share it, and the restraints imposed by counselling convention the more difficult to observe. Difficult, but immensely creative and the "meekness" involved, of holding the best gifts one has to give in restraint is central to godliness and Christ-likeness. Both the strength and meekness are essential to good counselling. Strength is needed for the helper, to give him endless staying power and faithfulness. But "meekness" of restraint of power is also crucial, to give those being helped ample and un-crowded space and all the time they need to come to their own unpressured appraisals of the truth for them, and to make free decisions in relation to it.

In the overt, verbal, explicit sense, this is "non-directive" counselling. Implicitly, it speaks volumes of wisdom. "Be patient with yourself, as I am. This world, unlike the one in which all the catastrophes were occurring that demanded snap decisions, is safe to take your time in. The grace and loving care around us now is greater by far than the grim terrors of foetal distress, birth trauma and the refusal to allow the baby to make the life-giving bond with the mother. These primal terrors need not now scare us into flight. I, or we (for in a Christian extended family or healing group this helping unit should be about 3 people), willing and deputed for the task, will be with you, strengthening the 'adult' you to reach down to and re-live the original fears." This is certainly not "non-directive" if that means, "When you have explored your own resources and those of your friends in the (at time rather aggressively) secular growth group, there is nowhere else to turn."

"Spiritual" Resources for Humanists

This defect has been, the humanist groups would say, remedied by the bringing to bear of a multitude of "spiritual resources" from the East, from "powers" made available by the rediscovery of ancient, and in certain times, contemporary, shamanistic disciplines, and in "psychosynthesis" from the philosophical knowledge, gnosis, or wisdom that was lost in the "scientific revolution". In my view there is more to caution than to commend in large parts of this development. It reaches into man, but when it seeks powers beyond him it readily puts itself under the influence and control of demonic powers, which then play havoc with his life in destructive ways he never bargained for. In leaving the way open to this grave misdirection, the "non-directive" humanist philosophy has, in my view, opened the gates, for some people, to delusion, insurgent evil and helpless personal tragedy. Their divisions are such that many of them would agree to that. When he comes into contact with this seduction, the Christian counsellor exerts every effort to warn against it. Where those who have been ensnared seek deliverance, he will bring together those to whom the Holy Spirit has given the gifts that make them competent to effect that deliverance by the authority and power of Christ.

Two models: Integrate vs. Cast Out

There is a radical change of model here, from the use of Christ's power to enable sufferers to **integrate** and become reconciled to primitive pain they could not bear on its first occurrence, to prayer that Christ will use His authority to **separate out** an oppressive or possessive power for which there is no remedy but to cast it out. It is important for the pastoral care-giver to discern which model he ought to be using. The fear engendered by foetal distress can be so overwhelming that the sufferer, but more frequently his spiritual guides, if they have no direct knowledge of the intensity of primal pain, will leap to use the use of the second model, thereby implying that there is a demonic element to be cast-out. This mis-diagnosis can add unnecessary fresh terrors to the sufferer's plight, particularly since the energetic attempts at exorcism do not work. There is no devil to be cast out. There is a scared foetal person who needs to be loved back into life and confidence. The pastoral counsellor needs the prayer group with the ministry gifts to check what may be an intuition of extraneous evil. They need him, for both elements are often present.

The Need for Confrontation

One of Carl Rogers most influential disciples, R.R. Carkhuff (1969), introduced a rigorous inquiry into what attributes in the counsellor reliably led to effective counselling. This is not the kind of analytic theory that leads to disputation. It is solidly and empirically grounded. We have used it as basic to our helper training for some years and have found it entirely satisfactory and Christianly valid. In our training, we spend time and effort in ensuring that we are able to know when we are offering these attributes and when we are not, and to sharpen our ability to offer them consistently.

The six attributes Carkhuff has distilled out, as present in effective counsellors, and absent in those who are ineffective or do their clients actual harm are (1) empathy, (2) respect, (3) genuineness, (4) concreteness, (5) confrontation, and (6) immediacy. While some of these bear more explanation (for instance immediacy and concreteness), what I am drawing attention to here is the appearance of the decidedly non-Rogerian attribute of effective counselling: confrontation. This is clearly NOT non-directive. It is saying, "Please look here. There is an inconsistency we must look at. Perhaps life doesn't actually work the way you want it to." Carkhuff has an absolute respect for honesty and work.

Those who want to "get by" in life without being honest with themselves and without contributing to the common responsibilities of work, cannot do it, nor will he help them to. If the whole project lacks truthfulness, and reality does not support it, it will not work.

Guile Must Go First

John Oman (1925) used to say that there is a necessary precursor, even to the action of God's redemptive grace in the soul. There has to be a prior diminution of the guile that so habitually distorts our perceptions. The Holy Spirit has to deal first with our refusals of insight. Our pride makes it difficult to admit where we have been wrong or seriously hurtful to others. Without honesty, no kind of growth into insight is possible, and without that, no glimmer of understanding as to what it is Christ offers can dawn on us, and no knowledge of who we are to whom He is offering it. So we are with Carkhuff here, for this is scriptural. And it was St. Paul who stated, peremptorily and bluntly, that "if a man will not work, neither shall he eat" (II Thessalonians 3:10).

7

Christ the Model:
The Dynamic Quadrilateral

Raising the issue of truthfulness means that we cannot escape facing up to the basic disclosure of revelation, that for Christians, Christ is the only adequate model for our humanity. He, and he alone, is what human beings are meant to be. If we want to know how our humanity is meant to work, which means the only way it will work, we must look more closely at Christ. The Scripture sets him forth clearly as the norm, the model. He is the Way, and insofar as we diverge from him, we have "gone out of the way" and are lost to the truth of our nature.

The Inner and Outer Dynamics of Jesus in St. John's Gospel

My wrestling with this problem of discovering a norm, as the baseline for all our work with human beings, in psychology, sociology, or any other related discipline, long antedated my entry into psychiatry. In the double appointment as Medical Superintendent and Lecturer in Parasitology at the Christian Medical College in Vellore, South India, I took part, as did all the staff, in weekly Bible Studies we offered to the students. My particular task was to compile a course on the integration of Christian faith and the personal aspects of medical practice. The obvious need was for a model of the normal. Aristotle says that if you intend to study the normal you must be careful that you are not examining spoiled specimens. Even among my most excellent friends I could not find any who did not regard themselves in all sorts of ways as "spoiled specimens". As a clinical pathologist I could distinguish the abnormal or diseased under the microscope, because I was thoroughly familiar with histology, with the appearance of normal and undamaged tissues and cells. But in the area of human studies, where was the histology? Where were the normal and unspoiled specimens?

In 1950, when spending a day with Emil Brunner, the Swiss theologian, who was on his way to Japan, I pressed him with this problem. He directed me to a sustained study of St. John's Gospel and the dynamics of the inner life of Christ as portrayed there, to see how he differed from the rest of us. This proved to be an astonishing revelation to me, and the key to my quest. I later realized how the three "fathers" of psychiatry, Freud, Adler and Jung, had dealt with this problem. Each had made "an act of faith", that it was legitimate on the basis of their extensive knowledge of patients (who would acknowledge themselves to be "spoiled specimens") to draw conclusions about human nature and what, at root, ordinary people were really striving for. Though it was certainly not characteristic of himself, Freud concluded that human beings, in the main, were striving for pleasurable sensations, curtailed only by the reality principle (Freud, 1955). This principle warned you not to steal other people's rights to their sources of delectable sensation, unless you were predictably able to supplant them. Adler, working in quite a different setting, with another class of patients, concluded that what the people he saw lacked was a sense of personal power. They suffered from "inferiority complexes". The one shared commonplace, he declared, "is the desire for power" (Adler, 1930). This is what the whole of human life is really striving for.

C.J. Jung, a totally different personality to the other two, seemed to escape from these body-and-matter-bound models of the norm into a model more spiritual, philosophic and within the mind, as man's "highest faculty". Aware of the amount of disturbance that derived from ill-balanced mental functions, he became convinced that what people really needed, if they wished to be wise and healthy, was inner knowledge (Jung, 1968). This became his norm and he lived dangerously to discover and communicate it in his many writings.

Pascal's Three Lusts

Given what Freud, Adler and Jung have written, I was startled to come across this pithy summary, in Blaise Pascal's *Pensees* (1958), of three ways of lusting for what the Scripture and Christ himself (as in his temptations) define as ways of taking flight from God. He says there are three lusts, using the Latin word "libido", for sensation, for power and for knowledge. As if to say, the first two are obvious, he adds, "and the philosophers have only chosen one of the three lusts" (p. 129). "Retire within yourself", say the philosophers, "and there you will find your rest" (p. 130). "And that," said Pascal, "is not true" (p. 130). All these things that I lust for become my possessions, a ground for security in myself, turning decisively away from any dependence on God and even on others, except for the sensation, power and knowledge they can give me. So far from defining normality, they define, in Pascal's Christian view, sin. Flight from what it is to be "normally" human characterizes them all.

Norms Are Held as "Acts of Faith"

Abraham Maslow had protested against the derivation of so-called normal psychology from psychiatrists' immersion in the deficiencies of their patients. He insisted that we should look for our norms, not by examining a sufficiently large number of sick and less sick specimens as to be statistically significant, but by looking closely at even a few men and women who have lived fulfilled lives (Maslow, 1968). What Maslow means by "fulfilled" may contain religious elements, but not essentially so. He remains within the humanist orbit. All these humanist attempts to define man in his normality are, without question, "acts of faith". It is high time for the Christian to say, "I also have made my act of faith in the normal man. His name is Jesus Christ of Nazareth, who died on a cross as a criminal and was raised from the dead to be the source of eternal life to all those who believe and trust in him."

Jesus' name for himself was "the Son of man". It is a vast leap of faith to say, of the whole world of human beings in their millions, as Emile Mersch (1938) did, "The manner of being that God willed for men was an *esse in Christo*, an existence in Christ....Human being viewed in its origins was in reality a supernatural being, a being of members destined to be joined together in a body: we have existence so that we can become members of the Saviour" (p. 22). Emile Mersch would have directed me, as Emil Brunner did, to St. John's Gospel, for he writes, "Throughout the Fourth Gospel we are put in contact with the very interior of Jesus, with his life, with his 'ego'" (p. 166).

Christ's Dynamic Requires Movement

In stark contrast to the way in which most human beings behave most of the time, and particularly when their defenses are working well, Christ showed a perpetual awareness of his Father's presence, and of his rela-

Illustration 1: The Dynamic Quadrilateral in the Life of Christ in relation, in turn to God as Father and to men in obedience to the Father, as a model or hypothesis for the analysis of the origins and development of "normal" healthy human personality structures and dynamic interactions (The references to chapter and verse are in St. Johns Gospel, unless otherwise stated)

PHASE I
ACCEPTANCE

Of Christ the Son by His Father; the voice of from heaven "This is my Beloved Son" (3:17; 17:5)

Christ's response to dependence as a Son and as a man, is to pray (Luke 6:12; 9:28)

He went up into a mountain to pray.

He is found alone, praying (Luke 9:18)

He faces crucifixion in the Garden praying

He knows that he has constant access.

"I know that Thou hearest me always" (11:42)

He is the only begotten Son of God the Father

This is his Being

John records that "I saw the Spriit descending from heaven like a dove, and it abode on   Him" (1:32)

PHASE IV
ACHIEVEMENT

This is strictly limited to the Father's will

"The Son can do nothing of himself but what he sees the Father do" (5:19, 30, 35; 8:29; 10:36-37)

"He can speak nothing of himself but what he hears from the Father" (8:26, 28, 38)

"The words that I speak they are spirit, they are life (6:63; 8:51)

"They are everlasting life to believers" (5:24, 40; 14:6)

He is the bread of life, of eternal life, for all who believe on, and eating, partake of him (6:48-58, 33-35)

To be the light of the world, so that those who follow Him do not walk in darkness (8:12; 9:5)

To finish the work of redemption, God gave him to do (4:34; 16:5; 17:4; 19:30)

"I must work the works of him who sent me while it is day (9:4)

PHASE II
SUSTENENCE

Christ abides in the Father.

His well-being derives from this

"The only-begottten Son which is in the bosom of the Father (1:18)

"As my Father has loved me, so I have loved you" (15:9)

The Father shows the Son "everything that He is himself doing" (5:20)

Christ is given the Holy Spirit and his gifts of love, joy, peace, patience, glory, all without measure (3:34)

"I am in the Father and the Father is in me" (14:11)

"I am my Father are one" 10:30)

PHASE III
STATUS

"I am from above" 8:23)

"I am the son of God" (10:36)

"I am not alone" (8:16-18;29)

He is sent by God on God's work (7:18, 28- 29, 33; 6:38)

"I am the light of the world" (3:19; 8:12; 9:5)

"I am the living bread come down from heaven (6:51)

"I am the water of life" (7:37)

"Full of grace and truth" (1:14)

Everything entrusted to him by God (Matt 11:27)

The Father is glorified in the Son (14:13)

Jesus said, "I tell you that in the future you see the Son of Man sitting at the right hand of power (Matt 26:64

Jesus commands men to leave all, take up your cross, and follow me (1:43; 12) tionship of loving dependence on him. In dynamic terms, Christ's life is dynamically on the move, whereas the natural man is standing on the same spot, collecting his supplies of sensation or power or knowledge, whatever his flesh, his eyes or pride lusts for, acknowledging no source or renewal of his being outside himself. When Christ withdraws from his self-giving service to the people round him, it is to move into the place of prayer. He moves away to some place where he will not be interrupted. There he knows he has constant access to the Father, "I know that thou hearest me always" (John 11:42). This constitutes his very being. Then there is, as part of this "input" phase a filling out of this, of sustenance, expressed by an affirmation such as "the only-begotten Son which is in the bosom of the Father" (John 1:18), with all that that image suggests of intimate supplying of every need. This is his well-being. When the voice from heaven spoke to announce who he was, there was first the plain statement of his identity, "This is my beloved Son . . .". Then it is clothed with feeling, warmth, tenderness and joy, " . . . in whom I am well-pleased" (Luke 3:22).

These, as we now know well, are the two basic questions which foetal persons ask of their maternal environment in the womb; the first, "Do you accept my presence here? Do you acknowledge me as yours? Have I any right to be? Can I count on you for being-itself". The second question includes, "Then if I am here, what does that mean to you? If I mean someone beloved, someone you are reaching out to so that I may respond with all my love-filled being, that gives meaning, glorious meaning and satisfaction to my being in you. In this sustaining and enfolding all my needs are met". Being-itself is raised to well-being.

These two aspects of the "input" phase are clearly distinguishable in St. John's account of the inner experience of Jesus. In this place of deep abiding, Christ is given the whole life of the Father, through the Holy Spirit who is given to him "without measure" (John 3:34). To us are given his endowments and gifts "by measure", to enable each of us to fulfill our place in the Body and its ministry. To the Lord himself, at this point the sole remaining representative of the faithful on earth, the "remnant", all the graces, fruits and gifts of the Spirit are given.

Sources of the Sense of Status

As decisively as Jesus moved away from involvement in the world, to prayer and abiding in the Father, so he moves back again, to the tasks that are there because of the needs of the people around him and of the disciples he is training. But before we see him actively engaged with people, we realize that it is important to him to say who he is, he who has just come out from the life of God to be life for the world. Under different images and metaphors he declares his status, his standing in the world because of the endowment of God the Father, totally centered in him. All the great "I am" statements gather here. "I am . . . the light of the world" (John 3:19; 8:12, 9:5), ". . . the living bread" (John 6:51), ". . . the water of life" (John 7:37). He knows that "all authority" has been given him in heaven and on earth. He has the power to heal the sick and raise the dead to life.

However, although all power, indeed "everything has been entrusted to him by God", this is immediately hidden and held in restraint as he begins to be with his disciples and the ordinary folk who gather round him. He presses his services on no one. Those who have deep needs, sorrows, weariness, humiliating weakness, or who suffer from social scorn because of their past lives, find him immediately at their side, drawing them into a loving fellowship, not with the religious establishment, but with a caring community along with others like themselves, with Jesus at the heart of it.

Achievement: Concentration and Limitation

So when we come to study the fourth phase of the dynamic cycle in the life of Christ, that of his achievement, we are impressed, not by its extensiveness, but by its astonishing concentration. All that he needed to show of the Father's nature, how he loved and to whom he could fully show that love, could be compressed into three years' ministry and recorded for us in a few stories out of many that could have been told. Yet we lack nothing of the essential portrait that we need to know.

In poring over the dynamics of the Son of Man in St. John's gospel I was riveted by the number of occasions on which he describes the curtailment of his activity, speech or action. Seven times he speaks of doing what he sees the Father do, or saying what the Father has for him to say. But fourteen times, in different ways, he insists also on the limiting counterpart. He "can do nothing of himself but what he sees the Father do" (John 5:19), and "can speak nothing of himself but what he hears from the Father" (John 8:28). "You go up to the feast", Jesus tells his disciples, "my time is not yet" (John 7:8). He responds to need, as in the evening at Capernaum when the whole crowd came for healing and were healed. But the next morning, when Peter caught him at prayer to say that more of the sick had gathered for healing, Christ had other plans for him that day, and so he and his followers moved on, away from the crowd (Luke 4).

These, then, are our grounds for discerning a four-fold dynamic cycle in the inner and outer life of Jesus Christ, the normal human being. He is the model for the well-functioning human person in relation to the source person who for him was his Father, God the Father. We have abstracted a theoretical model from his life, drawing attention to its twofold dynamic, that is to say, concerned with the flow of power, where it comes from and where it goes to, a division of input and output. Within each of these two phases we have discerned qualitative differences warranting further subdivision. Of what use is this? Have we not displaced the personal model God gave in his Son with an impersonal one which is bound to impoverish it? If we were displacing the personal model, this would be the case, and indefensible. What we are doing is reflecting on the personal to see what we may learn of the normal dynamics of human life, since, whether as professionals in health care, or as people responsibly involved in society in understanding what people do with personal power, where they drive it and how they dispose of it, we are constantly having to try to understand dynamic tangles.

The Deployment of the Model

Once you have derived your abstract model from the personal dynamics of the God-given pattern of the Son of Man, the question becomes, how far does the model apply as a way of understanding and analyzing (i.e. untying the knots in) other situations?

In his Bampton lectures on *Christian Theology and Natural Science*, E.L. Mascall (1956) writes: "The really useful models are those that are capable of wide 'deployment', that is to say, those which suggest further questions than those which they were originally devised to correlate and predict" (p. 63). Mascall cites Toulmin's *Philosophy of Science* (1953) where he "makes great use of the analogy of the map. He remarks how natural it is to speak of finding our way around a range of phenomena with the help of the law of nature, or recognizing where on the map a particular object of study belongs" (Mascall, 1956, p. 64). In the dynamic quadrilateral we have reason to believe that we have a "map", or a law of sequences, not of nature but of the divine nature manifest "in the flesh" as a human being, the model of what humanity is meant to be.

What follows is the map in its simplest form (see also Appendix 1: *The Basic Form of the Model* and Appendix 2: *The Ontological Model*).

Illustration 2: The Basic Form of the Model

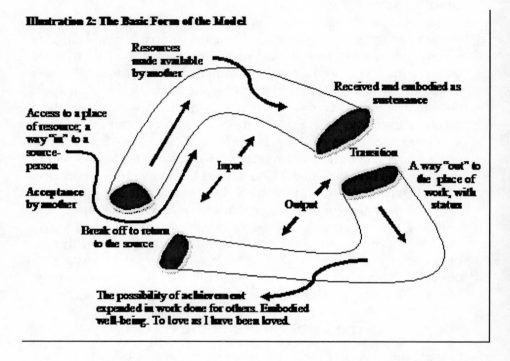

The question is, "Is this map or model capable of wider deployment than the purpose which inspired it, namely to understand the life of the Son of Man in dynamic terms?" If it does, we are helped. If it does not, no matter. There will be classes of phenomena to which it would be inappropriate to offer this map, this dynamic sequence of events, as a help in "finding one's way around". In fact, we have found it capable of very wide deployment, wherever human beings are relating to one another and transfers of power, or blockages in transfer or violations of transfer are taking place. For, of course, the exchanges of love are inextricably bound up with the way people use their power, in meeting, or refusing to meet, the needs of others for love.

Deployment as a Model of Maternal-Foetal Dynamics

I have already "jumped the gun" by remarking on the exact parallels between the first two phases, the need and gift of acceptance as a person, and of being filled out with an enveloping warmth and sustenance, and the regularly-heard appeals of foetal persons re-living the first trimester of their existence in the womb. They long for the messages that reassure them that their being there is recognized and fully accepted, and that that gift should be given meaning and satisfaction by the further messages of tenderness, commitment to sustain, and the offer of mutual love. If these are present, and I recall many foetal occasions when they have been, the sense of status, of who I am and of what value, rides high. With it come a zest for life and abundant motivational energy. It is a good world to be in, and good to be me within it. When such a foetal person encounters interruptions in this flow of input that meets all needs, as when the mother is temporarily distressed by some environmental mischance, it is immediately ready to cope with the change, confident in its basic security. It will achieve even an active sense of desiring to protect and care for the mother, free of any concern for itself.

The dynamic quadrilateral, in a most satisfactory sense, has been validly deployed. The good input is predictive of a high sense of status and eager achievement. That is the norm, what it ought to be like for all foetal individuals seeking to become well-related as persons of value to those from whom they seek these essential gifts, which passed between the Father and the Son.

The Marvelous Persistence of Foetal Hope

The absence of a welcoming maternal response to the pregnancy is, predictably, catastrophic for the foetus. The first law of human nature has been violated. It has no alternative means of coming to life in a satisfactory human way. The marvel we observe constantly is the persistence of the innate longing for recognition and welcome, despite daily silence from the mother or her outright rejection. This expectation can survive, though battered, baffled and discouraged, through the sharp distresses of the first trimester, through the perhaps grudging recognition of the rest of the pregnancy, and on through a babyhood and childhood that has little better to offer. Then at last through some Christ-like or Christ-filled offer of real acceptance and warmth, the long-hidden hope emerges, tentative at first but with growing confidence. It has been worth waiting for. "Though my mother could not accept or love me, I am loved here. I am a person and I am lovable". Although in that catastrophic first attempt to be, the evidence was unequivocal, "You are not lovable. You are worthless", "the message I longed for was just not getting through except as rugged hope God does love me. He gives me a right to respond to, and in responding, grow at last to the fullness of my powers."

How common or rare such phenomenal courage is, I cannot say. I do know that others are rendered bitter, full of hatred of a cruel and unjust world, and that they live on in a personality full of recrimination and hostility. Envy and jealousy grow in this soil. Others become resolutely self-destructive, turning all the rejections they have experienced upon themselves in "double-despair". They despair of the despairing self and with it a profound impatience, attack it and make as if to destroy it. Deadly addictions and suicides are common in such afflicted souls. There is an inevitable sadness now, in pointing out the predictive force of the model. Those who have been denied being-itself and well-being have no sense of personal status or the joy and zest that go with it. Nor are they able to flow into the achievement of loving service, either for themselves or others.

In 1966, in *Clinical Theology*, and in the years before and after its publication, we were alerted to foetal dynamics, and we saw and taught the applicability of the dynamic quadrilateral to the relationship of the baby to the mother in the "nursing couple". All this, of course, still stands. The chart entitled *The Womb of the Spirit* (See Appendix 3) is helpful in understanding what we originally proposed. It takes up the genesis of being itself, through the mother's gift of her countenance in unfailing recognition, and shows how the sustenance of being is raised to well-being. Through the mother's gracious and tender self-giving, an abundant, meaningful and satisfying self-hood is communicated, and is never lost whatever follows.

We reflected at that time on the likelihood that if the dynamic quadrilateral represented faithfully the relations between Jesus and his Father, those between Jesus and his mother, especially the vulnerability of his babyhood, should follow the same pattern as closely as possible. Bearing in mind her own holiness of character, manifest in her godlike identification with "the humble and meek", and her special endowment by the Holy Spirit for the mothering task, we had every reason to believe that this would be the case. As you read accounts of what good mothering does, which often survives in women living in otherwise disordered lives, it is not conceivable that the Blessed Virgin Mother would do less.

To this post-natal use of the model and our recognition that its requirement would be fulfilled, we have now added an awareness of the importance of Mary's giving to the foetal Christ the tranquility and security from disturbance, of which there was much on the way for Mary. But she wisely spent the crucial first three months in total peaceful seclusion with Elizabeth in the hill country of Judea, many miles away from Nazareth and Joseph and the gossiping villagers. So the requirements of the model based on the adult Christ are seen to have been fulfilled during the two earliest stages of human development, when Jesus himself would have been asking these questions, and receiving answers which reflect the message of Annunciation about him. Perfect exchanges of love are given and received. It is not, however, of unmixed bliss. This child is "the Son of God". He inherits an eternal kingship. Yet his name is Jesus, the Saviour, with all that means as a vocation to suffering.

The Womb of the Spirit

In giving the name "The Womb of the Spirit" to the nine months after birth, we used the analogy of the physical aspects of intra-uterine life, namely the utter reliance of the foetus on the intactness and unobstructed flow of oxygenated blood through the umbilical cord. The face-to-face, eye-to-eye bonding of the mother to the baby required the same intactness and total reliability. The analogy is still valid. The term "womb of the spirit" could now with more accuracy by transferred to the earlier developmental state, within the first half of the nine months of pregnancy which are the crucial ones, though extending throughout pregnancy until birth. While the roots of major neuroses, hysterical, phobic, conversion, schizoid, anxiety depressive and obsessional disorders may arise from severe deprivation of the mother's presence in the post-natal period, our evidence from the twelve hundred or more subjects who have re-lived foetal distress in the first trimester would appear to indicate that the main roots of these disorders must occur in the first part of pregnancy and not later.

The Virtuous Vice

Input must always be the precursor to output. But for many, this is difficult because they feel in a way virtuous to be spending themselves unstintingly on others and neglecting themselves. Comfort comes from, "It is more blessed to give than to receive", which is bad advice for such people. The Christ-model insists that there is no more or less "blessed" in either. When the Father calls you to replenish your life in him, it is more blessed to be praying, to be receiving. When he calls you to pass on his life to your neighbours, it is more blessed to be obeying, with the giving that this involves. It is particularly difficult to overcome this virtuous vice because it usually has firm foetal roots. With great frequency we hear foetal persons who are aware that their mothers are too exhausted or distracted to give them the acceptance and sustenance which they need. They have resolved to set aside their own needs and live by the fantasy that they are thus helping their mothers. This is indeed a fantasy. They are giving out of a heroic sense of dedication, not anything substantial, but eager intentions to be of service in ways that are as eager as they are impractical. This foetal heroism, martyrdom even, feels so virtuous, at such a depth, that to accept correction, even from Christ and the Spirit, feels to be throwing away a good resolution and its reward. This is one of the many places where foetal resolutions or "scripts" collide with the realities of Christian obedience. One has to give way. It has been of great help, to those who have re-lived the force of this foetal dedication to a fixated attitude of always giving, to recognize its origin, its "validity" then, and its total invalidity now. The break is made with no regrets. The challenging norm, throughout, comes from the model of Christ, who did not neglect prayer for more service.

Predictive Deployment in Childhood

The predictive value of the quadrilateral is put to work when we ask, for instance, if this five-year old child, on the first day of school, is to go home at night with a sense of status and happiness at achieving some of the tasks of settling in, what will be necessary at the acceptance and sustenance phases? The answer, of course, is a sense of full and unconditional acceptance by the teacher, that you now belong here as a right, and some quite personal assurances of warmth, kindliness, particular care and liking. These give meaning and graciousness, satisfaction as well as sustenance.

The Womb as an Institution

Here, too, there are strong foetal resonances. Becoming aware of existing in the womb as an embryo is rather like being placed in an institution. There are no ready-made friendships but you desperately hope to make one. When the mother's recognition and loving tenderness begin to get through, the bare walls cease to be unfriendly and threatening. The model infers that, as with Jesus coming to awareness in Mary, God's desire and plan is that women liable to become pregnant should live in a constant attitude of acceptance and sustenance of whoever may be "on the way". This often does not happen in the womb so that institutions become places where more than usual care needs to be exercised to ensure that new arrivals are welcomed and oriented by the unmistakable holding of at least one pair of kindly eyes, one warm voice that speaks your name with affection and hands that fit round your shoulders. If this happens, status and achievement will surely follow. If not, they will be lacking.

Does God Feel Like an Institution?

To many people, God feels more like an institution than a person. They are quite unsure of themselves in a vast and quite impersonal "vault of heaven". It seems very doubtful that the great "It" should have anything to say personally to them. The ultimate reassuring sayings of Jesus about "Abba", Dear Father, strike no chord of resonance within them. It is not until some real person, with eyes and face, voice and hands, brings the Father and Jesus vividly to life in a human way, that it begins to dawn on them that there are presences and voices speaking to them personally. These are the deployments of the model. The quadrilateral, then, is a close study of one input-output dynamic sequence as it goes on in the experience of one individual.

Conclusion

Grounding the Dialogue

Reading again Sebastian Moore's *The Fire and the Rose are One* (1980) and his forceful search into what constitutes for the human being his essential questions, to others and to "God", by the hearing of answers to which he could know himself to enjoy self-hood and worth, constantly one wants to cry out, "Exactly dear Brother, how accurately and persistently you pursue these questions. Can you look at your inquiry again and recognize that these are not primarily urgent questions asked by babies and infants of their parents, nor 'mystical' questions asked by the soul of God, but are the questions constantly being asked by the foetal person, of 'the Beloved' it profoundly longs will be there, to give recognition and being, to convey meaning, worth and well-being, but who so frequently is incapable of giving, or even considering the possibility of giving, either?" It is here, in the findings from the first trimester, that the transposition of the language and context of the dialogue needs to take place, if the diligent researches of such profound students of origins as Rosemary Haughton (1981), Sebastian Moore (1980) and Rowan Williams (1982) are to come to rest where they actually belong.

There is no discipline exploring man's "existential" personal roots, his identity and self-hood, which would not come alive with recognitions once the richness of the foetal dialogue with the mother, or the devastating lack of it, is taken seriously. A new sureness will come to existential enquiries and answers about the "at present" hidden origins of our human being, when this is done.

The Matrix of Mythology

Humankind used to keep a kind of contact with these "unconscious" conflicts through its mythologies. These have still their ancient power, though among moderns their practical effectiveness is largely lost. Anthropologists from Ernest Becker (1962; 1964; 1969) on, some philosophically-minded analysts, and now some powerfully perceptive Christians, have returned to the quest, sensing man's "lostness" just at this central issue of identity and meaning. I have a solid conviction, that grows as I reread their writings, that I have now spent over four years, dealing with all these crucial questions, and here is the crux, at the precise stage in their human development when human beings begin to ask them and require answers, namely in the three months following conception.

To make this claim has ceased to be the bold advancing of a hypothesis. It is a firmer and better-integrated paradigm (or major model or pattern) for the interpretation of all that concerns psychodynamic origins and spiritual roots, than anything I have known in a long medical and psychiatric life that is now drawing to a close.

Appendix 1: The Basic Form of the Model

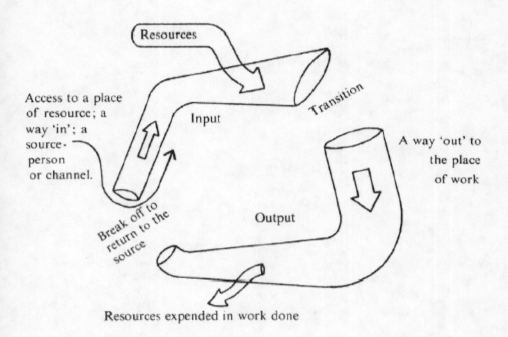

Resources

Access to a place
of resource; a
way 'in'; a
source-
person
or channel.

Input

Transition

A way 'out' to
the place
of work

Break off to
return to the
source

Output

Resources expended in work done

Appendix 2: The Ontological Model

The sources of personal 'being-itself' and of 'well-being' are
opened by love and care, acceptance and sustenance given by
the source person, who goes 'down' to draw the needy one
into being-by-relationship, and then opens up rich communicable
personal resources. These, responded to, complete the 'input'.
A strong sense of status, and identification motivates a
movement to give out to others. The achievement of this
service is the output.

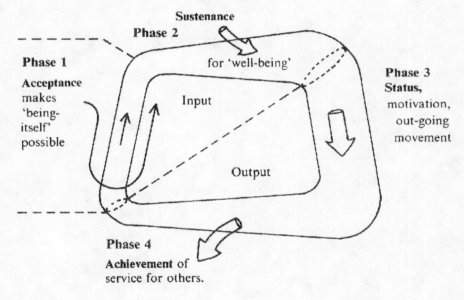

Appendix 3: The Genesis of Being

APPENDIX 3. N. b. 1. 'The Womb of the Spirit'. An Ontological Analysis of the normal Mother-Child relationship: The dynamics of the nursing couple. This model suggests a dynamic framework of understanding of the normal (i.e. 'unspoiled', rather than 'average') Mother-Baby relationship. It draws full attention on the recorded pattern of the life of Christ, interpreted in interpersonal dynamics. Assuming HIS Mother-Baby relationship to have been of the same basic pattern, we propose its use as a dynamic model or ontological norm.

TRANSITION

from life-by-identification to awareness of separateness

1 The Genesis of BEING. The Formation of 'I-my-self'

The Dynamics of the origin of the human spirit in the 1st year

The RESPONSE to the Mother's Person, by which the child achieves the status of a person. In the first NINE months, more or less, of life outside the physical womb, the infant is still within the 'Womb of the spirit'. The baby has no capacity for separate personal existence. It can conceive of itself as 'in Being,' or Alive, only by identification with the Mother's Being and Person. The dichotomy which later distinguishes the boundaries between the baby's 'I' and the Mother's 'Thou', is not possible at this stage. The ANALOGY of the growth of the body in the womb is an apt one. Personal or spiritual Being is the result of nine months, (more or less) response of the baby to supplies of personal or spiritual being from the Mother. The 'umbilical cord' or relational element, by which this spiritual being passes to the baby, is subserved by ALL the sensations of Mother's presence, especially by SIGHT. The baby comes into being as a person, gains selfhood and the sense of identity by responding to the light of her countenance. If all goes well, at the end of about nine months, the

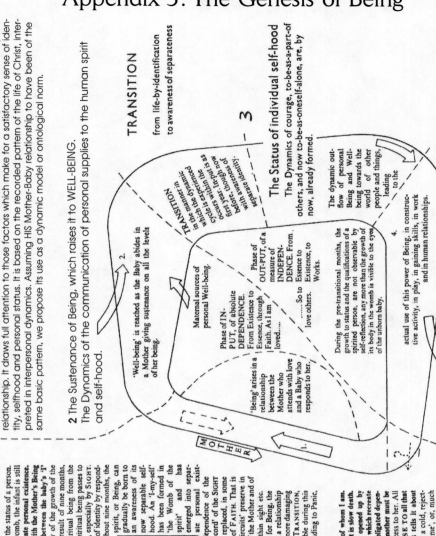

spirit, or Being, can gradually be born to an awareness of its now separable selfhood. An 'I-my-self' has been formed in 'the Womb of the spirit' and has emerged into separate personal existence. The obligated dependence of the baby on the 'umbilical cord' of the SIGHT of the Mother is now replaced, in some measure, by the 'cord' of FAITH. That is to say, reverberating circuits preserve in the mind a firm sense of the Mother and of

1. Mother Special sense and Distance Receptors especially SIGHT.

1. Mother. Physical Being is the result of nine month's response by the foetus to the supplies of physical Being from Mother. If 2. is constricted, the foetus will become distressed;

2. The Baby is only a term of a relationship.

Life is only in the triad.

if blocked, it dies. If all goes well, at the end of nine months the foetus can be born; a dichotomy is possible; an 'I-my-body' is born. Separate physical existence is a fact.

1. Mother.
2. Placenta and Cord.
3. Foetus is only the third term of a relationship.

one's secure relatedness to her, even when she is not actually within sight etc. Mother has 'substance' though not seen. Still dependent on Mother for Being, the mode of dependence is no longer by identification (monistic), but in a relationship of two persons; a duality. Therefore Separation-Anxiety is infinitely more damaging and productive of personality distortion and neurosis before the TRANSITION, while still in the 'identified' period. The spirit is specifically vulnerable during this symbiotic phase to periods of painful longing endured passively, leading to Panic, then worse, to Dread.

ACCESS to the SIGHT of Mother is access to Life, to knowledge of whom I am. The Infant's Being lives in the light of her countenance. To be shut out is slow death. THE WAY IN to right-relatedness to oneself, in this phase, is opened up by Mother's return; the LOOK in her eyes and the SOUND of her voice, which recreate Belongingness. ACCEPTANCE by the Mother, of this close and obligated dependence of the baby, is essential to its Being. This incorporation by the mother must be unconditional, 'As of right', the baby should be given priority of access to her. All that the baby can bring is need of her, trust in her, i.e. a RESPONSE TO all that the LIGHT OF LOVE and acceptance and welcome IN HER EYES tells it about itself. Patients under L.s.d. remember feeling almost annihilated by a cold, rejecting, 'you're-hopeless' look, or by a Mother who did not notice me', or, much worse, did not come at all. Passively constituted infants did not cry in protest. It was inferred that Mother knew of the pain she was causing by remaining absent. **The roots of all the major neuroses, hysterical, phobic, conversion, schizoid, anxiety depressive, and obsessional, derive from Separation-anxiety incurred in this phase.**

2 The Sustenance of Being, which raises it to WELL-BEING.

The Dynamics of the communication of personal supplies to the human spirit and self-hood.

'Well-being' is reached as the Baby abides in a Mother giving sustenance on all the levels of her being.

Maternal sources of personal Well-being.

Phase of IN-PUT, of absolute DEPENDENCE. From Existence to Essence, through Faith. As I am loved.....

Phase of OUT-PUT, of a measure of INDEPEN-DENCE. From Essence to Existence, to Works. ......So to love others.

'Being' arises in a relationship between the Mother who attends with love and a Baby who responds to her.

TRANSITION

in the manner in which the experienced cycle within is as occurs in-put is as now first year, though of before, though with awareness of separate identity.

The Status of individual self-hood.

The Dynamics of courage, to-be-as-a-part-of others, and now to-be-as-oneself-alone, are, by now, already formed.

During the pre-transitional months, the growth to status and the qualifications of a spirited person, are not observable by self-reflection, any more than the growth of its body in the womb is visible to the eyes of the unborn baby.

The dynamic outflow of personal Being and Well-being towards the world of other people and things, leading to the

actual use of this power of Being, in constructive activity, in play, in gaining skills, in work and in human relationships.

4 Achievement. The Dynamics of work,

References

Adler, Alfred (1930). Individual psychology. In C. Murchison (Ed.). *Psychologies of 1930.* Worcester, Ma.: Clark University Press.

Balint, Michael. (1965). *Primary love and psycho-analytic technique.* New York: Liveright Publishing.

Balint, Michael, (1957). *Problems of human pleasure and behaviour.* London, Hogarth Press.

Balint, Michael. (1968). *The basic fault: Therapeutic aspects of regression.* London: Tavistock Publications.

Balint, Michael. (1959). *Thrills and regressions.* New York: International Universities Press.

Becker, Ernest. (1969). *Angel in armor: A post-Freudian perspective on the nature of man.* New York: G. Braziller Books.

Becker, Ernest. (1962). *The birth and death of meaning, a perspective on the nature of man.* New York: Free Press.

Becker, Ernest. (1964). *The revolution in psychiatry: The new understanding of man.* New York: Free Press.

Blake, William, & Emery, Clark Mixon. (1966). *The book of Urizen.* Coral Gables, Fla.: Univ. of Miami Press.

Bowlby, John. (1969). *Attachment and loss.* New York: Basic Books.

Bowlby, John. (1980). *Loss: Sadness and depression.* New York Basic. Books.

Bowlby, John. (1973). *Separation: Anxiety and anger.* New York: Basic Books.

Bowlby, John. (1979). *The making and breaking of affectional bonds.* New York: BasicBooks.

Carkhuff, R.R. (1969). *Helping and Human Relations.* New York: Holt, Rinehart & Winston.

Dollard, John, & Miller, Neal E. (1939). *Frustration and aggression.* London: Oxford University Press.

Dollard, John, & Miller, Neal E. (1950). *Personality and psychotherapy.* New York: McGraw-Hill.

Dryden, Richard. (1978). *Before birth.* London: Heinemann Books.

Fairbairn, W. Ronald D. (1954). *An object-relations theory of personality.* New York: Basic Books.

Fairbairn, W. Ronald D. (1952). *Psychoanalytic studies of the personality.* London: Routledge & Kegan.

Freud, Sigmund. (1955). Beyond the pleasure principle. In J. Strachey (Ed. & Trans.). *The standard edition of the complete works of Sigmund Freud* (Vol. 18). London: Hogarth Press.

Guntrip, Harry. (1961). *Personality structure and human interaction: The developing synthesis of psycho-dynamic theory.* New York: International Universities Press.

Guntrip, Harry. (1971). *Psychoanalytic theory, therapy and the self.* New York: Basic Books.

Guntrip, Harry. (1969). *Schizoid phenomena, object relations, and the self.* New York: International Universities Press.

Haughton, Rosemary. (1981). *The passionate God.* New York: Paulist Press.

Herbert, George (1941). *The works of George Herbert.* Oxford: The Clarendon Press.

Hopkins, Gerard Manley. (1967). *The poems of Gerard Manley Hopkins.* (W.H. Gardner & N.H. Mackenzie, Eds.). London: Oxford University Press.

John of the Cross. (1949). *The complete works of St. John of the Cross.* (E. Alison Peers, Trans. & Ed.). Westminster, MD: Newman Press.

Julian of Norwich. (1966). *Revelations of divine love.* New York: Penguin Books.

Jung, C.G. (1968). *Analytical psychology: Its theory and practice.* New York: Pantheon.

King, Truby (1940). *Feeding and care of baby.* Christchurch, NZ: Whitcombe & Tombs.

King, Truby (1919). *Natural feeding of infants.* Auckland, NZ: Whitcombe & Tombs.

King, Truby (1924). *The expectant mother and baby's first month: For parents and nurses.* London: Macmillan.

Kierkegaard, Soren. (1946). *Fear and trembling* and *The sickness unto death.* (Walter Lowrie, Trans.). Princeton, NJ: Princeton University Press.

Kierkegaard, Soren. (1941). *The concept of dread.* (Walter Lowrie, Trans.). Princeton, NJ: Princeton University Press.

Kierkegaard, Soren. (1938). *The journals of Soren Kierkegaard: A selection edited and translated.* (Alexander Dru, Ed.). London: Oxford University Press.

Klein, Melanie. (1948). *Contributions to psycho-analysis, 1921-1945.* London: Hogarth Press.

Klein, Melanie. (1957). *Envy and gratitude: A study of unconscious sources.* New York: Basic Books.

Klein, Melanie. (1975). *The psycho-analysis of children.* New York: Delacorte Press.

Lake, Frank. (1966). *Clinical theology.* London: Darton, Longman & Todd.

Lake, Frank. (1981). *Tight corners in pastoral counselling.* London: Darton, Longman & Todd.

Lake, Frank. (1982). *With respect: A doctor's response to a healing pope.* London: Darton, Longman & Todd.

Lowen, Alexander. (1975). *Bioenergetics.* New York: Penguin Books.

Mascall, E.L. (1956). *Christian theology and the natural sciences.* London: Longmans Green & Co.

Maslow, Abraham H. (1968). *Toward a psychology of being* (2nd ed.). New York: Van Nostrand.

Mersch, Emile. (1938). *The whole Christ.* London: Dennis Dobson Books.

Moore, Sebastian. (1977). *The crucified Jesus is no stranger.* New York: Paulist Press.

Moore, Sebastian. (1980). *The fire and the rose are one.* New York: Seabury Press.

Oman, John. (1925). *Grace and Personality.* New York: The Macmillan Company.

Pascal, Blaise. (1958). *Pensees.* New York: E.P. Dutton & Co.

Pavlov, Ivan P. (1927). *Conditioned reflexes: An investigation of the physiological activity of the cerebral cortex* (G. V. Anrep, Trans.). London: Oxford University Press.

Pelletier, Kenneth R. (1978). *Toward a science of consciousness.* New York: Delacorte Press.

Perls, Fritz. (1973). *The gestalt approach and eyewitness to therapy.* London: Bantam Books.

Robertson, James, & Robertson, Joyce. (1989). *Separation and the very young.* London: Free Association Books.

Robertson, James, & Robertson, Joyce. (1982). *A baby in the family: Loving and being loved.* New York: Penguin Books.

Robertson, James, & Robertson, Joyce. (1971). Young children in brief separation: A fresh look. *Psychoanalytic Study of the Child, 26,* 263–315.

Tolkien, J.R.R. (1954a). *The fellowship of the ring: Being the first part of the lord of the rings.* Boston: Houghton Mifflin.

Tolkien, J.R.R. (1955). *The return of the king: Being the third part of the lord of the rings*. Boston: Houghton Mifflin.

Tolkien, J.R.R. (1954b). *The two towers: Being the second part of the lord of the rings*. Boston: Houghton Mifflin.

Toulmin, S. (1953). *Philosophy of science*. London: Hutchinson.

Weil, Simone. (1951). *Waiting for God*. New York: Harper & Row.

Williams, Charles. (1961). *Selected writings*. (Anne Ridler, Ed.). London: Oxford University Press.

Williams, Rowan. (1982). *Resurrection: Interpreting the Easter gospel*. London: Darton, Longman & Todd.

Winnicott, D. W. (1958). *Collected papers: Through paediatrics to psychoanalysis*. New York: Basic Books.

Winnicott, D. W. (1964). *Mother and child: A primer of first relationships*. New York: Basic Books.

Winnicott, D. W. (1957). *The child and the family: First relationships*. London: Tavistock Publications.

Winnicott, D. W. (1965). *The Maturational processes and the facilitating environment: Studies in the theory of emotional development*. New York: International Universities Press.

Wojtyla, Karol. (1979). *Easter vigil and other poems*. New York: Random House.

Subject Index

A

Afflicted 41-42, 52, 63-67, 73-74, 100
Affliction(s) 12, 23, 30, 42-43, 50, 52-53, 66, 73, 76
Attached 46
Anxiety/anxious 15, 18, 36, 49, 68, 80, 84, 101

B

Baby/babies 15-16, 22-23, 34, 53-57, 62, 73, 78-79, 81, 88, 100-101, 105
Babyhood 48, 99-100
Beloved 49, 67, 72, 79, 95, 105
Bio-feedback 35-37
Birth 11, 13, 15, 18, 21, 23, 28, 35, 37, 48, 54-56, 59, 69, 73, 78, 81, 88, 101
Blastocyst 28, 33, 46, 56-57
Bond(ing) 22, 29, 34-35, 45, 52, 88, 101
Brain 27-28, 35, 37, 55, 75
Breath/breathe/breathing 16, 33, 35-36, 46

C

Child(ren) 13, 37, 47, 65, 68-69, 75, 77-78, 80-81, 85-86, 101-102
Childhood 13, 15, 48, 69, 76, 99, 102
Christ 1, 13, 16-17, 19, 23, 27, 42, 64, 66-72, 77-78, 86-93,95-99, 101-102
Christian 1, 9, 13, 17, 19, 21, 42-43, 52, 64, 66-71, 80, 87-89, 91, 93, 97, 102, 106
Clergy 85
Clinical Theology 9, 21, 51, 100
Clinical Theology Association (CTA) 12, 15
Community 17, 19, 29-30, 42, 51, 68, 70, 84, 96
Conception 17-19, 21-22, 24, 29-30, 34, 37, 39-40, 44, 54, 72
Conscious(ness) 9, 13, 21, 29, 35-37, 43, 54-55, 63-64, 67, 69, 74

Sin(s)/sinner/sinful 13, 63-68, 71-72, 93
Social worker(s) 18, 40, 85
Somatic 749
Soul(s) 23, 73, 76, 90, 100, 105
Sperm 34
Subconscious 35
Suffering(s) 12-13, 25, 38, 42, 52, 56, 6

T
Teacher(s) 40, 83, 102
Theodicy 61, 77
Therapist(s) 40, 49, 85
Theta 35-37
Tight Corners in Pastoral Counselling 11, 15
Time(s) 12, 16-17, 19, 24-29, 34, 37-38, 40-41, 43, 45-48, 50, 53, 55-58,
    62-67, 69-71, 75, 78-79, 81, 83, 86-89, 93, 96, 100
Transmarginal 21-22, 26, 50-51, 53-56, 73, 77, 81
Trauma/traumatic 15, 25, 54-55, 69, 88
Trimester 11, 13, 15-16, 21, 23-25, 29, 34, 45, 48-49, 53-55, 59, 64, 73-
    81, 99, 101, 105
Trust 26-27, 35, 38, 76, 93

U
Umbilical 23-24, 34, 46, 48-50, 56, 74-75, 101
Unconscious(ness) 18, 26, 29-30, 35-37, 45, 69, 105

W
Wisdom 47, 80, 83-88
With Respect 15
Womb(s) 15, 21, 46, 48, 53, 56-58, 69-70, 73, 76, 78-80, 95, 99-103
Workshop(s) 11, 16, 18, 27, 29-30, 34, 39-40, 45-46, 53

Z
Zygote 28-29

Name Index

A
Adler, Alfred 92

B
Balint, Michael 22
Bernanos, George 69
Bowlby, John 22
Blake, William 52
Brunner, Emile 92-93

C
Camus, Albert 24
Carkhuff, R.R 89-90

D
Daniel 58
Dollard, John 21
Dryden, Richard 28

E
Elizabeth 78-79, 101

F
Fairbairn, W. Ronald 22
Freud, Sigmund 86, 92

G
Guntrip, Harry 22

H
Haughton, Rosemary 77, 105

Bible Passage Index

For Further Reading and Investigation

Bridge Pastoral Foundation (formerly Clinical Theology Association). http://www.bridgepastoral.org.uk

Frank Lake (n.d.). Retrieved March 20, 2008, from Wikipedia: http://en.wikipedia.org/wiki/Frank_Lake

House, S. (2000). Primal integration therapy: The school of Dr. Frank Lake. *Journal of Prenatal & Perinatal Psychology & Health, 14*(3), 213-236.

Lake, F. (1969). *Birth trauma, claustrophobia and LSD therapy.* Retrieved from the Primal Psychotherapy Page Web site: http://primal-page.com/lake.html

Lake, F. (1966). *Clinical theology.* London: Darton, Longman & Todd.

Lake, F. (2006). *Clinical theology, a theological and psychiatric basis to clinical pastoral care* (Vols. 1-2). Lexington, KY. : Emeth Press.

Lake, F. (1991) *In the spirit of truth: A reader in the work of Frank Lake.* (C. Christian, Ed.). London: Darton, Longman & Todd.

Lake, F. (1987a). *Personal identity: Its origin.* Birmingham, UK: CTA/Bridge Pastoral Foundation (Lingdale Paper #6).

Lake, F. (1987b). *Personal identity: Its development.* Birmingham, UK: CTA/Bridge Pastoral Foundation (Lingdale Paper #7).

Lake, F. (1986). *The dynamic cycle: An introduction to the model.* Birmingham, UK: CTA/Bridge Pastoral Foundation (Lingdale Paper #2).

Lake, F. (1998). *The first trimester.* (David Wasdell, Ed.). London: URCHIN.

Lake, F. (2000). The theology of pastoral counseling. In D. Willows & J. Swinton (Eds.). *Spiritual dimensions of pastoral care: Practical theology in a multidisciplinary context* (pp. 127-135).

London: Jessica Kingsley Publishers.

Lake, F. (1981). *Tight corners in pastoral counselling.* London: Darton, Longman & Todd.

Lake, F. (1988). *Transferences in pastoral care.* Birmingham, UK: CTA/Bridge Pastoral Foundation (Lingdale Paper #9).

Lake, F. (1966). The sexual aspects of personality. In H. Montefiore (Ed.). *We must love one another or die* (pp. 11-47). London: Hodder & Stoughton.

Lake, F. (1982). *With respect: A doctor's response to a healing pope.* London: Darton, Longman & Todd.

Maret, S. (1996). Frank Lake's "dynamic cycle". *Stulos Theological Journal, 4,* 65-74.

Maret, S. (1995, April). Frank Lake's "theology of correlation". Paper presented at the Eastern Regional Meeting of the Evangelical Theological Society, Phoenixville, Pa. Retrieved from the Theological Research Exchange Network http://www.tren.com/e-docs

Maret, S. (1992). *Frank Lake's maternal-fetal distress syndrome: An analysis.* Ph.D. dissertation, Drew University, Madison, NJ.

Maret, S. (Speaker). (2007, February). *Frank Lake's prenatal personality theory.* Paper and speech given at the APPPAH International Congress, Los Angeles, Ca., (CD Recording 7PPN-31) from http://www.birthpsychology.com/congress/07ORDERCDsVicki.html

Maret, S. (1997, March). *The prenatal life of Christ: A consideration of the writings of Frank Lake and Pope John Paul II.* Paper presented at the Eastern Regional Meeting of the Evangelical Theological Society, Hatfield, Pa. Retrieved from the Theological Research Exchange Network http://www.tren.com/e-docs

Maret, S. (2001). *The prenatal person: Frank Lake maternal-fetal distress syndrome.* Lanham, MD. University Press of America.

Moss, R. (1987). Frank Lake's maternal-fetal distress syndrome: Clinical and theoretical considerations. In T. Verny (Ed.). *Pre- and perinatal psychology: An introduction* (pp. 201-208). New York: Human Sciences Press.

Moss, R. (1986). Frank Lake's maternal-fetal distress syndrome and primal integration workshops. *Journal of Prenatal & Perinatal Psychology & Health, 1*(1), 52-68.

Nelson, P. (1976). *The clinical theology of Frank Lake: critique and evaluation.* Unpublished master's thesis, Trinity Evangelical Divinity School, Deerfield, Il.

Oden, Thomas C. (1983). *Pastoral theology: Essentials of ministry.* San

Francisco: Harper & Row.

Peters, J. (1989). *Frank Lake: The man and his work*. London: Darton, Longman & Todd.

Ross, A. (1994). *An evaluation of clinical theology*. Oxford: CTA.

Speyer, J. (n.d.). *The Origins of the Fear of Death and Dying in the Writings of Frank Lake, M.D.* Retrieved from the Primal Psychotherapy Page Web Site http://primal-page.com/lake.html

Whitfield, G. V. (2007). *The prenatal psychology of Frank Lake and the origins of sin and human dysfunction: Its relevance for the pastor and psychotherapist*. Lexington, KY.: Emeth Press.

About the Author

Frank Lake was born on June 6, 1914 in Lancashire, England, and eventually attended Edinburgh University. While there he committed himself to become a medical missionary to India. As he studied for his medical degree, he also trained with the Church Missionary Society and attended theology lectures. It was during this time he met his future wife Sylvia Smith and became engaged to her prior to heading off to India in November 1939.

He served at several missionary hospitals in India and in 1944 Sylvia joined Lake in India, where they were married, and their son David was born. In 1946 Sylvia returned to England to give birth to her daughter Monica. Lake followed in 1948, but after a year of furlough, returned to service in India alone to become the medical superintendent of the Vellore Christian Medical College. It was here that he met and was profoundly influenced by two people, the theologian Emil Brunner, who challenged Lake to come up with a model of human functioning based on the person of Jesus in the gospel of John, and Florence Nichols, who introduced Lake to psychodynamic psychiatry.

Lake returned to England in 1950, where his daughter Marguerite was born and he began retraining in psychiatry. During this period, while at Scalebor Park Hospital in West Yorkshire, Lake interacted with and was profoundly influenced by Harry Guntrip, an influential member of the Object Relations School. It was also at Scalebor that Lake spent almost 2 years experimenting with the use of LSD as a therapeutic tool.

In the latter part of the 1950s, Lake began to realize that in his interaction with clergy, there appeared to be a severe lack of both understanding and training in psychological theory and technique. Because this greatly hampered the clergy's ministry to troubled parishioners,

133

Lake decided to address this lack by organizing "clinical theology" seminars for clergy. The eventual result was the founding of the Clinical Theology Association (now the Bridge Pastoral Foundation) in 1962. These integration seminars of psychiatry and theology for clergy also provided the grist for Lake's 1200-page book *Clinical Theology,* which was published in 1966 and reprinted in 2005 by Emeth Press.

It was during the last several years of his career that Lake began to articulate and write about what he saw as his most important discovery, the influence of the prenatal period on subsequent psychological functioning. This "Maternal-Fetal Distress Syndrome" was to be the topic of his final three books. Lake died of cancer in 1982, just one month after finishing *Mutual Caring*.

About the Editor

Stephen Maret was born in Somalia and spent his childhood in Ethiopia as the child of evangelical missionaries. He has also previously lived and worked in Japan, South Korea and St. Croix.

He received his Ph.D. and M. Phil. degrees from Drew University in psychology and theology, where he was introduced to the work of Frank Lake by his advisor, Dr. Thomas Oden. He wrote his doctoral dissertation on Frank Lake's Maternal-Fetal Distress Syndrome and has continued to write and lecture on Lake's contributions to pastoral care, theology, counseling, and prenatal psychology.

He served as an assistant pastor for 8 years at Calvary Church in Essex Fells, NJ and has held professorships at Nyack College Manhattan and Caldwell College in Caldwell, New Jerseu and was a visiting professor at Duksung University in Seoul, South Korea. He is the author of many articles as well as several books, including *The Prenatal Person* and *Introduction to Prenatal Psychology*. He is the married father of 2 young adult children and resides in New Providence, New Jersey.

LaVergne, TN USA
12 July 2010
189238LV00004B/53/P